'The Stonebreaker' John Brett A.R.A.

BOX HILL

Geoff Chapman & Bob Young

SERENDIP

First published in 1979
by Serendip Fine Books
Lyme Regis, Dorset, England

Designed by Mike Frost
Typeset and printed in Great Britain by
Penwell Ltd, Parkwood, Callington,
Cornwall

ISBN 0 9504143 1 X

CONTENTS

Foreword

Chapter

FOREWORD

Our first chapter makes it plain that we have been helped, directly and indirectly, by a large number of people in writing our book. It would be impossible to thank them all individually but we would like to assure them of our gratitude.

Our very special thanks are due to Dr. T. Gascoigne who drew the two diagrams of orchid parts for us. We are proud to have had the generous help of so able and distinguished a scientist. We are also very grateful to Mr. J.H.P. Sankey, sometime Warden of Juniper Hall Field Centre, now Liaison Officer to the Field Studies Council, for valuable advice and permission to refer to his excellent little book "Chalkland Ecology".

Thanks are also due to Mike Frost for the delightful illustrations of wild life and flowers and for the map and cross section which he drew from our rough sketches.

The reproduction of "The Stonebreaker" by John Brett, A.R.A., is by permission of the Walker Art Gallery, Liverpool. Painted in 1857-58, it is not only a magnificent work of art but is intensely interesting in showing how little Box Hill has changed in 120 years. The portraits of Fanny Burney, Jane Austen, Keats and Meredith are reproduced with the permission of the National Portrait Gallery. With the exception of the four photographs taken by Mike Frost the illustrations are all from photographs taken by ourselves.

We would like to express our indebtedness to several books which we frequently carried with us on our walks on Box Hill and which greatly helped us to a fuller appreciation of the richness and variety of its wild life. In particular we would mention "Wild Flowers of the Chalk and Limestone" by T.E. Lousley, "Wild Orchids of Britain" by Professor V.S. Summerhayes, "London's Countryside" by Professor S.W. Wooldridge and G.E. Hutchings, and "The Book of Box Hill" by G.E. Hutchings.

We wish to thank the Librarians of the Bodleian Library at Oxford for providing facilities for research for our literary chapters; in particular for the opportunity to read all the 18th century volumes of the Gentleman's Magazine.

To the publishers of certain books from which we have quoted we extend our thanks: to Messrs. Methuen for permission to quote from

"With a Spade on Stane Street" by S.E. Winbolt and "The Dancing Bees: An Account of the Life and Senses of the Honey Bee" by Karl von Frisch, English translation by Dora Ilse; to Messrs. Constable for permission to include several extracts from "The Old Road" by Hilaire Belloc; and to Messrs. Cape for permission to quote from "Talleyrand" by Duff Cooper.

Where names of orchids are concerned we have followed Professor Summerhayes' nomenclature; for the names of other wild flowers Messrs. Collins' well-known Field Guide. The spelling of place names is that observed on the Ordnance Survey maps.

Box Hill attracts in many ways, not least by its changelessness. You go there to escape from the hubbub of London and to seek the peace of the everlasting hills. You look at centuries old trees and at a forest that has endured since Stone Age times. Yet, like all natural environments, Box Hill is continually changing in minor details. Thus readers may find their experiences differ from ours. They may find more or less Roman snails or glow-worms, larger or smaller numbers of whitethroats or fragrant orchids, more or fewer "swallow holes" in the bed of the Mole between Burford Bridge and Leatherhead. We hope that readers of our book will find it interesting to compare their own observations with ours.

G.M.C.   R.H.D.Y.

CHAPTER ONE
BOX HILL. PLAYGROUND OR SANCTUARY?

There can be no better known nor better loved hill in the country-side around London than Box Hill. Leith Hill, Ashdown Forest, Chanctonbury Ring, Ivinghoe Beacon, to name but a few rivals, will all have their champions, but if a poll were to be taken it is odds-on that more people would have heard of or know Box Hill than any of these others. For two or three centuries it has been a haven for people seeking to escape from the stuffiness of summer in London. The arrival of the railway train, and later the motor car, made it a popular resort for all manner of folk, from day-trippers to anglers and naturalists. Though not very high in comparison with other hills not far away, it dominates the landscape in a way peculiar to itself. Belloc described it as "the strongest and most simple of our southern hills." Therein perhaps lies the secret of its appeal, for strength and simplicity conjoined create beauty.

We knew the hill well and loved it, which is why we have written this book in praise of it. Over a period of twenty-five years it was our constant haven. We went there chiefly during evenings in mid-week throughout the summer, though sometimes we would go for whole days at any time of the year. Only August, the school holiday month, is a blank in our diaries. Together as a rule but sometimes singly, each of us has made over three hundred visits to Box Hill and the surrounding locality.

The book we have written is really an escape story — escape from a noisy, crowded city to a green solitude of cool woods and wind-swept downs, bird song and flowers, where a little river runs beneath the massive hill and the cloud shadows straddle the Weald between Box Hill and Chanctonbury Ring. Escapes are often achieved by prosaic means. The suburban trains of the Southern Electric system, rattling past Sutton and Epsom, would deposit us at Box Hill quite early in the evening. This meant that, in the summer months, with the aid of summer-time, we had nearly five hours of daylight before us. It is easy for a pedestrian of no more than average powers to walk in that time from Box Hill Station to the top of Box Hill and over Headley Heath and return with time for a snack and a pint at the Burford Bridge Hotel or the Stepping Stones Inn before catching a train home. Sometimes the walk might be in the opposite direction, up the valley through West Humble to Polesden Lacy and back by

Ranmore and Denbies, with its splendid views from Denbies Scarp, over Dorking, to the slopes of Leith Hill. In the height of summer, when the daylight lasts longest, one can go on to Dorking and walk over Holmwood Common, listening to the nightingales, or take the bus from Dorking to Wotton and return to Box Hill through Deerleap Wood and over White Down, to see the flowers in their midsummer glory. A shorter walk we sometimes took is that which follows the path by the Mole to Leatherhead. Or we might ramble through the Norbury woodlands and make our way back by way of Phenice Farm, where Fanny Burney and General D'Arblay spent their honeymoon.

But most of our evenings were spent on Box Hill itself. The place has some special blend of light and colour, some particular arrangement of woods and brushy thickets, deep-cut combes and grassy hill-tops, which make it almost impossible to resist. As the train rounds the curve beyond Leatherhead, with the tree-lined course of the Mole on the left, the long wooded crest of Box Hill comes into view. Once through the tunnel by which the line traverses a spur of the hills which form the western side of the Mole valley, one sees the steep, grassy slope which rises above Burford Bridge and the hanging woods with the familiar bare chalk patches of the Whites, dropping sharply to the river-side meadows. Individual trees can be seen now, standing burnished and solid above their shadows in the afternoon sunlight. It is a prospect which brings an immediate uplift of the spirit and instant release from the cares of everyday life. It re-awakens delight in the natural world of flowers and birds, trees and grass, sunlight and cloud shadow. That is why we spent most of our evenings on Box Hill itself and why this is really an escape story. On summer evenings we usually had the place more or less to ourselves, which heightened the feeling of escape from the city, where the rush-hour would be at its peak. It is only at week-ends that Box Hill becomes crowded.

Not that we had set out in any misanthropic frame of mind. Even in comparatively lonely places the people who do actually live there are the people who make the place and cause one either to linger or to hurry away. Here, at Box Hill, the reception is tolerant and friendly. The staff at the railway station, the ladies in the tea kiosk, the taxi lady from West Humble, the hosts and barmen at the Stepping Stones and Burford Bridge Inns, the succession of proprietors of the Fort and Swimming Pool and Box Hill Cafés, the wardens and staff of the Juniper Hall Field Centre, the bus drivers who steer the single-deckers from Leatherhead to Headley, or the double-deckers from Leatherhead to Dorking, the farmers of Bradley and Warren Farms, the foresters and water bailiffs, the National Trust car-park wardens, the riding-school instructors, the caravan and camping-club officials, above all the patient police who shepherd the sometimes unruly hordes of day visitors — all these live in the area and make most visitors welcome.

One thinks too of men and women who lived long ago and whose lives and work were of importance in the evolution of the landscape which gives us such pleasure today, for it is man-made as far as its superficial features, its farm-lands, formal estates, woodlands and open areas of heath and sward are concerned. The people who laid the foundations of the landscape of Box Hill as it is at present include such men as Sir Cecil Bishopp, who bought the Juniper Hall estate sometime towards the middle of the eighteenth century and began the planting of the trees which add so much to its elegant beauty, and Mr. Broadwood, a later owner of Juniper Hall, who used some of the money he accumulated from the sale of his pianos in further improvements. Other land-owners were carrying out similar work on near-by estates at the same time, notably at Denbies and Polesden Lacy, across the valley from Box Hill. Not to be forgotten either are the farmers who cultivated the fields and the shepherds who minded their flocks on the downs. Their names may be forgotten but their work lives on for us to enjoy today.

Box Hill is certainly a place for the people, as it has been for three hundred years. The drifts of youths are always there on summer week-ends. Whether they call themselves teds, mods, rockers, greasers, skin-heads, shed boys, hell-fire clubs, bad men of Tombstone City, ton-up boys with their Nazi accoutrements, the lingo changes but the phenomenon is the same. It is the result of an abundance of energy, a burning desire to *be* someone, and to escape from London. There are bathers and anglers, family parties, Boy Scouts, pony trekkers, naturalists in pursuit of butterflies, flower-plunderers, pedal cyclists and motor cyclists and motorists, storming the Zig-zag. There are carefully posed actresses, advertising automobiles against a scenic background. There was once a temporary prison camp film-set on Headley Heath for some episode we never witnessed, and for another, an Afghan cardboard castle which bobbed up over-night like a mushroom at the first zig in the Zig-

Zag. There was a cavalcade of actresses and actors in their coaches enacting the picnic scene in Jane Austen's "Emma". In winter, given half a chance with snow, Box Hill becomes a winter sports centre. Toboggans, sledges and tin trays, skiers and sitting-glissaders career down the slopes above Burford Bridge, producing clients for the waiting ambulances and police cars on the Mickleham Road. In heat-waves people bask in the sun on the escarpment or plunge into the swimming pools. Box Hill, like the Malverns of Piers Plowman, provides a vision of a "Fair Field Fulle of Folke". For the wild life of the area, one of the main themes of this book, such teeming multitudes, were it not for three considerations, would provide a problem indeed.

The first of these considerations is that most people are as gregarious in their habits as the gannets on Ailsa Craig. The area around the Salomon Memorial and the southerly slope below it may be swarming with humanity, but remoter parts of the hill remain comparatively deserted. Secondly, unless a three or four day week becomes the rule, it is only at the week-end that the playground aspect of Box Hill is dominant. For five days of the week Box Hill is still a sanctuary. The third, and by no means the least consideration, is that more than five thousand acres of this part of the Surrey country-side are in the possession of the National Trust, or form the subject of protective covenants between the owners and the National Trust. Under the Trust's guidance and the constant surveillance of that hard-working body "The Friends of Box Hill", the grosser forms of pollution or of commercial development are prevented. Thus a remarkable number of mammals and birds, trees and flowering plants, continues to survive in Box Hill the Sanctuary. Survival of wild life is also indirectly aided by the appeal of the panoramic view from the top of Box Hill. Many people go there to gaze across the Weald to Chanctonbury on the South Downs or, from the northern side of the hill, to Windsor Castle on the edge of the Thames. While they are admiring the further land-scape, the nearer inhabitants, be they foxes or grasshoppers, can go about their business undisturbed and in comparative safety.

In this book 'Survival' is another main theme. We show, by comparing our records, made over twenty years, which species have survived and which are in perilous decline; which have adapted themselves to changing conditions; which are flourishing and which have become extinct. It is our belief that, while Box Hill is certain to

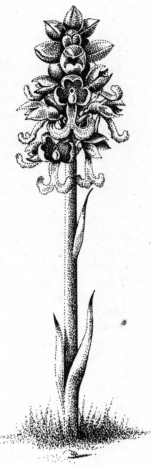

Bird's nest orchid

survive as a playground, it may remain a sanctuary as well. Rare plants do indeed survive there; orchids, bee, fly and man, bird's-nest, fragrant and musk, some of them fortunately mistaken for grasses, still bloom; autumn ladies' tresses seem almost to have adapted themselves to the trampling of many feet. These orchids are as numerous now as they were in the nineteen-fifties. Mammals still dwell on Box Hill: foxes, badgers and the survivors of the once ubiquitous rabbits. Shy birds still survive in the quieter parts of the area while others, such as the Wood Warbler, which no longer breed

11

on Box Hill, at least re-visit their old haunts from time to time. Insects such as the six-spot burnet, the common blue and the soldier beetle, can still breed here, un-menaced by crop-spraying helicopters.

Survival unfortunately cannot be taken for granted. The action of man on his surroundings has sometimes the same effect as the blight cast on the ground by the drippings in the shade of a tree. By dint of extreme specialisation or, alternatively, by developing a wide adaptability, some species of animal, bird or plant finds a way to live with man, but the casualties are many. More species of birds have disappeared from Box Hill in the last twenty or thirty years than have appeared. Nightingale, Nightjar, Woodlark, Wood Warbler and Red-backed Shrike have retreated to less frequented localities or gone altogether, though sometimes for climatic or ecological rather than man-made reasons. It is no compensation that there are more wood pigeons and starlings, or that collared doves and harlequin ducks have joined the list of breeding species in the area.

Box Hill as a sanctuary sometimes leads a precarious existence. No single action of man in the 1950's had so much effect as the introduction of myxomatosis into the rabbit population. Compared with the decimation of the rabbit and the resulting conversion of much of the chalk sward into impenetrable jungles of dogwood and thorn scrub, the other interferences of man have had small effect — even the trampling by thousands of walkers along the well-worn routes and the ensuing denudation of the grass down to the underlying chalk. Outside National Trust areas, crop-spraying, hedge-removal, ribbon-development housing and the building of motor-ways and arterial roads, have all upset the ecological balance, but not so catastrophically as the disappearance of the rabbit. Kestrels seem to have adapted to the thunder of traffic along the motorways to their advantage, by pouncing on mice or worms that surface in dismay at the din! Similarly other species have altered their habits to their own benefit on Box Hill. One has only to think of the numerous birds which hang around the cafés soliciting tit-bits from the customers.

Changes there must be, of course; some good, some not so good. Sheep now graze on Box Hill, as they did in time gone by, introduced as an experiment by the National Trust. They should be of benefit to the downland sward and may even, by nibbling back the encroaching scrub, once kept down by the rabbits, reverse some of the adverse effects of myxomatosis. On the other hand a craze for dry tobogganing is causing serious erosion of the grass on the steeper slopes while hang-gliding has, predictably, made its appearance. Recently a new form of pressure has appeared in the hordes of motor-cyclists who use Box Hill as a rendezvous. Other innovations will inevitably materialise, arising from the restless ingenuity of those who are forever seeking new ways of occupying their leisure time. All no doubt, increase the appeal of Box Hill the Playground while imperilling Box Hill the Sanctuary. Damage caused by the elements, such as that resulting from the severe winters of 1947 and 1962-63 is made up naturally in a few years. Species which were wiped out locally, like kingfishers, grey wagtails, green wood-peckers and wrens, eventually move back into the area; but were it not for the wise policies of the National Trust and other organisa-tions with similar aims there would be far less chance of countering the worse effects of man's presence, and less chance of avoiding that human tendency, castigated by Tacitus, of making a 'Desert' and calling it 'Peace'.

Most of Box Hill is owned, as has already been said, by the National Trust. It stands in the centre of a remarkable concentration of Trust properties, many of them visible from the crest of the hill. If the covenanted properties are added, the total area under the Trust's protection amounts to about 5000 acres. It is not therefore surprising that one so frequently comes upon the National Trust's emblem, the acorn and oak leaves, on their metal plaques, on and around Box Hill.

The most recent development in the long history of Box Hill as an open space dedicated to the enjoyment of ordinary men and women is the designation of the top of the hill as a Country Park. The idea of the Country Park was first suggested by the Countryside Com-mission, an official body operating under the Department of the Environment. This new status conferred upon Box Hill perpetuates an old and nearly forgotten tradition. Many years ago, at holiday times, the space between the Box Hill Road and the trees which shelter the Fort Café used to be crowded with swings, round-abouts and side-shows. It must have resembled a miniature Hampstead Heath at Bank Holiday time. This open space was known as Donkey Green, probably because donkeys were provided for children to ride. Sometime later Donkey Green became a cricket field. In fact, for something like three hundred years, Box Hill has been a popular resort for the Londoner on holiday. Once excursion trains carried him there, though only as far as the station of course, leaving him to toil, with his family or girl-friend, up the steep ascent from the Mickleham Road. Nowadays car and motor-cycle are the chief means by which he arrives, conveying him direct to the top of the hill. On the occasions when the railway still brings day trippers, the steep slope above Burford Bridge is liberally sprinkled with the recumbent figures of those who have decided that enough is enough and Box Hill can wait until they have got their breath back.

Of course Box Hill will remain a playground. So long as the National Trust can preserve it against exploitation and pollution it can remain a sanctuary as well. But is it misanthropic to be mildly sad at the changes? The Box Hill of 1950 already seems remote. The Box Hill of Meredith and Fanny Burney seems infinitely further away. Almost the only common factor now remaining is the Box Tree, which, though no longer grown as a commercial crop, still flourishes as it did in their day. We can, at least, describe for our successors in loving detail, some of the lovely things that grew and lived upon Box Hill in our day. We describe the Sanctuary. The Playground we leave to others.

CHAPTER TWO
GEOLOGY AND SCENERY OF BOX HILL

South-east England has not always been as we see it today. In fact, most of the features with which we are familiar and which have such an appearance of age-old permanence — downs and Weald, sea-cliffs and valleys — are not much over one million years old, a mere trifle of time, geologically speaking. Few of them are more than three million years old.

The explanation of this is that, during the last three million years or so, the area which is now western Europe, including the British Isles, has undergone a series of slow elevations. As these took place it requires little imagination to realise that the rivers would cut their valleys steadily deeper into the slowly rising land. As they did so the land between the valleys of the rivers would become more and more prominent, eventually forming ridges or lines of hills. In south-east England two such ridges are the North and South Downs. Another is the line of sandstone hills known as ragstone in Kent and the Surrey sand hills further west. Leith Hill, in this ridge, is well known as the highest point in south-east England. (The geologists' name for this rock is Greensand, a somewhat misleading term derived from the fact that, when the rock is first exposed to the air in quarrying operations, it is pale green in colour owing to the presence of the mineral glauconite. This speedily oxidises and turns to the normal brown or yellow-brown of this rock as one sees it in the field.)

In olden times people were puzzled by the fact that the rivers had penetrated the chalk ridges of the North and South Downs. They thought the Downs had always been there and could not understand how the rivers, confronted by a wall of solid chalk, had managed to get through it. They decided that they must have burrowed their way through. This was partly responsible for the legend of the under-

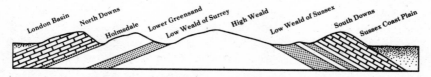

CROSS-SECTION NORTH TO SOUTH THROUGH S.E. ENGLAND
Clays and sands shaded dark; chalk shown by blocks; lower green-sand and Central Wealden rocks unshaded.

ground course of the Mole, of which more will be said in a later chapter. What actually happened was that, where the course of a river crossed the line of one of the rising ridges referred to above, it naturally had to cut itself an ever-deeper valley. Thus the Mole and other tributaries of the Thames have cut narrow gorges in the chalk of the North Downs ridge. Rivers flowing into the Channel have cut similar gorges in the South Downs ridge.

The gap through the North Downs, cut by the Mole, is about four miles long. It runs from near Dorking to Leatherhead. Many people consider it the most beautiful of the gaps cut by the Wealden rivers in the Downs. It is marked by a feature unique in south-east England. This is the magnificent river cliff which rises abruptly from the banks of the Mole where it runs through the meadows at Burford Bridge. The reason why the Mole gap alone amongst the river gaps of south-east England is dominated by such a feature appears to be the fact that the Mole approaches its gap from the east, running for a mile or so along the narrow vale known as the Holmsdale, below the scarp of the Downs. This has the effect of tying the river, so to speak, to the foot of the great chalk bastion of Box Hill. The Mole can never swing away westwards as it does elsewhere in its gap, with the result that the river saws unceasingly at the base of Box Hill. One can observe the process quite easily in a stroll through the meadows at Burford Bridge. On the steep eastern slope, above the river, a series of little shutes will be noted, descending from the precipitous heights of the Whites. At the bottom of each of these shutes a little delta of chalk rubble and flints projects into the river. The shutes are made, not, as might be thought, by small boys scrambling up the hill or sliding down it the hard way, though no doubt they help, but by material loosened by the under-cutting action of the river tumbling down under the influence of gravity. Occasionally a tree, undermined in this way, falls into the river, bringing earth and stones with it.

Smaller river cliffs can be found elsewhere in the Mole gap, for example at Ham Bank and Cowslip Bank. But these the river has abandoned from time to time in the past as its meanders swung from side to side of the gap. The great cliff of the Whites however, it can never leave. It is tied to it for ever because of the easterly sweep of the Mole along the Holmsdale.

The Holmsdale is itself an interesting feature. One sees it well from the crest of Box Hill, a long, narrow and straight vale, running

right: Bee Orchid.

below: The Ashurst Valley;
a typical bee orchid location.

Box Hill from Ranmore.

Box Hill; the Playground. *above:* View from the Salomon Memorial, probably the best known spot on Box Hill. *below:* Winter sports on the slope above Burford Bridge, 1963.

Box Hill; the Sanctuary. *above:* The almost inaccessible wooded river cliff above the Mole. *below:* The entrance to Juniper Bottom with White Hill beyond.

Two approaches to Box Hill. *above:* The steep track leading uphill from Burford Bridge. *below:* The Headley Lane.

Geoff Chapman writes notes on the slope below Juniper Top.

Bob Young on the way to Juniper Top.

above: The track to the crest from Burford Bridge, plainly showing the erosion caused by heavy use. *below:* View east from Betchworth Clump.

above: The scarp face of Box Hill east of the Salomon Memorial, with a glimpse of the Weald beyond. *below:* Juniper Top, part of the level plateau which lies back of the scarp crest.

west between the Ranmore scarp and the lower slopes of Leith Hill, east between the ramparts of Colley Hill and Betchworth Clump and the greensand ridge at Reigate. Holmsdale means the vale of the holly trees, holm being the old English word for the holly, as in holm oak. It was once thickly forested and presumably holly trees were numerous there. It is now largely meadow and coppiced woodland, with few dwellings on its heavy, often water-logged, soil. Barely one field in width, it marks the outcrop of a narrow seam of a blue-black clay called Gault, between the chalk and the sandstone ridges. Small streams, such as the Pipp Brook, which flows through Dorking, and the Tillingbourne, descending the dip slope of Leith Hill, turn west or east along it to join the main streams, the Mole and the Wey. It is these little streams which have excavated the vale. It therefore provides a good example of the influence of the geology on the scenery of the Wealden area. It is due to the erosion of the clays of the Holmsdale and the Weald itself that the chalk and sand-stone ridges so dominate the landscape.

Clay of a different type from that of the Weald or the Holmsdale is found, surprisingly enough, on the top of Box Hill. A walk through Ashurst Rough, the woodland on the top of the hill, in any but the driest weather, quickly convinces one that he is not treading on chalk. The ground is heavy and sticky. Pools of water often lie upon it and one's footwear speedily becomes clogged with a peculiarly adhesive brownish-yellow clay. It is known as Clay-with-Flints. Should one come across an excavation in it one sees that it is well named for the clay is full of flints. One can also see that it is a com-paratively shallow deposit, unlike the Gault and the Weald clay, which are deep. It is rarely more than twenty feet in depth. There has been much controversy over the origin of this clay, which is found not only on the tops of the North Downs but on those of the western Chilterns. It is possible that it is a relic of the various clays and sands which still lie over much of the lower part of the London Basin and once extended much further up the slopes of the North Downs and the Chilterns from which they have been removed by erosion. The flints in it come of course from the under-lying chalk.

Another and more interesting superficial deposit found on the chalk is the sand and gravel of Headley Heath. Here one could easily imagine that one is walking over a sandy sea-shore. Nor would this be by any means an erroneous impression for these sandy deposits are relics of a shallow sea which ebbed away as the land rose slowly upwards in the manner described in the beginning of this chapter. The waves of an ancient sea did, in fact, once break here upon their sandy beach. It is not difficult to find big flints which have been rounded by the action of these waves.

Another interesting fact about the sandy deposits on Headley Heath is that they lie at approximately 650 feet above present sea level. This provides a measure of the amount of uplift which the land has undergone since it first began about three million years ago. It is impossible to over-estimate the importance of this uplift in the evolution of the landscape we see around us today. Every single feature of consequence in it results from this slow emergence of the land from the sea. The shaping of the landscape has however, been done largely by the rivers. Given increased erosive power because of the uplift, they proceeded to excavate the great lowland of the Weald, the narrower lowland of the Holmsdale and the gaps in the chalk ridges by which they make their way to the Thames and the Channel. Without these two processes, working in harmony, there would have been no Box Hill, no river cliff, no Headley Valley, no Juniper Top, nor any other of the familiar features with which this chapter is concerned.

One other feature of the landscape deserves to be explained because it is possibly the most important in respect of the contribution it makes to the beauty of the scenery. It is also important because of the richness of its plant, bird and animal life. This is the system of dry valleys or combes which lies to the north of the scarp of Box Hill. It is largely responsible for the character and peculiar charm of the place. There are six of these combes on Box Hill. From west to east they are, the Zig-Zag, Juniper Bottom, the Ashurst Valley, a small un-named combe and the two combes which lie west of Headley Heath and meet just below Wentworth Hall. All of these combes run down to the Headley Valley. This valley begins below Headley village and joins the valley of the Mole not far from Mickleham. There is a marked dip in the road to Mickleham, opposite to Juniper Hall, which indicates its course. A similar system of combes lies north of the Ranmore scarp of the Downs. These combes run down to the Polesden Lacy valley which corresponds with the Headley Valley on the opposite side of the Mole.

Though they are now devoid of running water it does not take more than a cursory glance to realise that these combes are water-cut. Travelling down the Headley Valley one can easily believe that it was once occupied by a stream. The smooth curves, inter-locking spurs and gentle slopes on the south side, are obviously the same as those of any normal river valley. There is even an old river-cliff, like a small version of that of Box Hill itself, opposite to Warren Farm. The combes running down the north side of Box Hill are equally obviously water-cut. They once held tributaries of the stream which flowed down the Headley Valley. To walk up Juniper Bottom is, without any doubt, to walk up an ancient water course. It is so plainly a water-cut valley that one finds oneself looking and listening for the missing stream, surprised that it is not there. Surely, one thinks, it cannot be far away. It must be over there concealed by those tall grasses? Or there, below those over-hanging trees? But the sight and sound of water are both absent from the valley now. Only in times of heavy and continuous rain will a short-lived torrent appear, rushing down the narrow, upper part of the valley, where it commences, on the edge of Ashurst Rough.

Various explanations have been suggested for the disappearance of the streams which cut these combes. The lowering of the water-table* in the chalk, resulting from the slow erosion and consequent deepening of the Holmsdale, is one. This would have caused the springs which once fed the brooks in the combes, to dry up. Another possibility is that the rainfall was heavier in the past. This would have resulted in a higher water-table in the chalk, giving rise to springs feeding streams which cut the combes. Rainfall is known to have been heavier towards the close of the Ice Age than it is now. During the Ice Age itself water in the chalk would have been frozen, with the effect of making the rock impermeable. Surface water, resulting mainly from the melting of some of the snow and ice in summer, would have been unable to sink into the chalk as it does to-day. Instead it would have formed streams which would have excavated valleys for themselves in the frozen ground. As the country south of the Thames lay beyond the ice-sheets which covered the rest of the country, no permanent ice lay there, though there were probably small local ice-caps on the higher ground. In the brief summers there might have been enough melt-water flowing from these to cut valleys in the frozen chalk.

The explanation of the presence of these dry valleys in the Downs

* A somewhat confusing term which means simply the level in the rock below which it is saturated with water. At this level springs are likely to emerge where the water-table intersects the slope of the ground.

may be, as with many geological problems, a combination of the various suggested solutions. The really important fact is that they are there, for they endow the landscape with great beauty as well as providing sanctuaries for wild life, the badgers, birds, orchids and other lovely wild flowers, butterflies, moths and all those humbler yet none the less delightful creatures, such as the big Roman snails, which one finds in them.

The importance of the Ice Age in the evolution of the scenery of Box Hill, already seen in the origin of the combes, is evident also in the Mole valley. Stand on the little hill called the Nower, south of Dorking, and you will see, to the north, where the Mole enters its gap, a gently sloping shelf of ground extending towards the river at Pixham. It can easily be made out for it comprises the bulk of the fertile fields of Bradley Farm. It is a portion of the pre-Ice Age floor of the valley of the Mole. Today it lies at about 200 feet above sea-level. The present floor of the Mole valley at this point is some 100 feet lower. During the Ice Age the Mole must, therefore, have lowered its valley by this amount, being enabled to do so by the slow uplift of the land already described. The Ice Age Mole, swollen with melt-water from the ice, must have been a larger and more turbulent river than the placid little stream of today, endowed with much greater erosive power. It is fascinating to try and visualise the landscape as it may have been at that time. It must have been a dreary, tree-less place of bare chalk rock, tundra and snow-fields, swept by blizzards, the home of musk oxen and the wolves which pursued them, the Mole a grey torrent in summer, a river of ice in the long winter. It is difficult to suggest a landscape with which to compare it. Perhaps it looked something like the interior of Iceland does at the present.

The landscape of Box Hill and the Mole valley today is a gentle one. It has no straight edges, no jagged outlines, no trace of harshness. This is due largely to the nature of the chalk rock. Chalk is a form of calcium carbonate and is therefore soluble in rain water which, as it contains carbon, is, in effect, an extremely dilute solution of carbonic acid. This slowly dissolves the chalk so that all rough edges are gently smoothed away, producing a landscape of soft and regular curves, pleasing and satisfying to the eye.

The chalk has other qualities which go far to making it unique amongst the rocks of the British Isles. One is its dazzling whiteness, so well seen in the cliffs of the Channel coast. Another is its fertility.

This is, at first sight, surprising, for the soil which lies upon it is so thin that one can push the blade of a penknife through it almost anywhere except in the valley bottoms, to the solid rock. Its surface is littered with flints and the fragments of flints, broken and split by frost. Yet despite the thinness and stony character of the soil the trees, grass and wild flowers which grow in it do so luxuriantly. This is partly because there is always moisture in the porous rock. Chalk rarely dries out. Thus the short, sweet grass of the downs nearly always appears green and healthy. There is also some quality in the rock which gives to the numerous wild flowers which grow on it a brilliance of colouring not seen in the flowers of other rocks with the exception of those which grow on the mountain limestone of the hills of the north and west (itself a form of calcium carbonate). W.H. Hudson, in "A Shepherd's Life", remarks on this characteristic of the chalkland flowers: "All colours and all sounds have a purity and vividness and intensity beyond that of other places" he wrote, and went on to list some of the flowers in which it was particularly noticeable — hawkweed, rock-rose, birdsfoot trefoil, milkwort, squinancywort and dwarf thistle.

Hilaire Belloc is another writer who loved the chalk. In "The Old Road" he writes "The chalk should somewhere be warmly hymned and praised. (It) filtered our drink for us and built up our strong bones; . . . the chalk is our landscape and our proper habitation . . . The chalk gives a particular savour to the air." The truth of the last of these observations is well known to those who love the chalk country. Its scent is unmistakable though difficult to describe. It is a sharp, pungent, slightly sour yet pleasing aroma, partly emanating from the rock itself, partly the aromatic fragrance of the flowers which grow upon it, thyme and wood-sage, marjoram, wild basil and others, some of which are as familiar to the cook as the botanist.

It may be true that, as Belloc suggests, the chalk has some health-giving property not found in other rocks. To walk upon it induces a feeling of well-being, just as the aspect of the landscape produces an uplift of the spirit. Wherever in England one comes upon the chalk, whether it be that of Kent or Sussex, Dorset or Wiltshire, or even that small portion of it which lies in East Devon, one feels at once a peculiar contentment of the mind such as no other type of country bestows unless it be the limestone. Not only is there the same familiar sharp, clean scent, but the same communities of trees and flowers growing upon the pale grey earth, so that however far from Box Hill one may be, one feels amongst old friends.

It is interesting to speculate on the particular physical character-istics which have made Box Hill one of the best-known and best-loved places in the British Isles. Foremost amongst these is its situation in relation to adjacent features of the landscape. These are all tributary to Box Hill, leading the eye to it, the central point in the scene. Belloc compared it to a cape, jutting out into the Weald as into a sea. He pointed out how it conceals the slopes of the downs beyond it so that "it occupies the landscape alone". There are no minor features to distract the eye from the great mass of the hill. It stands by itself, a single elementary feature.

Two other characteristics which help to make the hill unique, at least in South-east England, are its perfect proportions and faultless beauty of line. Seen from the crest of Ranmore its profile is one of great simplicity, convex in its upper half, concave in the lower. Belloc wrote "Something of that economy and reserve by whose power the classic in verse or architecture grows upon the mind, is present in the North Downs." What Belloc said of the North Downs as a whole applies with particular force to Box Hill. It is a simple piece of landscape which can be sketched in one single flowing line of the pencil. Because of this simplicity it conveys a sense of perfect harmony, extremely satisfying to the mind so that one never tires of gazing at it.

Just as celebrated as the prospect of Box Hill itself is that from its crest. It is one of the best known views in Britain, if not in the world. We have many memories of this magnificent view, in widely differ-ent conditions of weather and at all seasons of the year. One may serve to illustrate them all. We had reached the crest of the hill one evening shortly after a July thunderstorm had rolled overhead. The westering sun had appeared as the rags of the departing storm streamed away behind us. The Weald was spread before us like an illuminated map, woods, villages, church spires, all clear and dis-tinct, up to the sun-lit forested ridges of the High Weald. Beyond these the South Downs were sharp against the rain-washed blue of the sky, Chanctonbury Ring and Ditchling Beacon discernible in unusual detail. To the west great floods of golden light streamed into the Holmsdale and the entrance to the Mole gap. The Ranmore scarp, with the spire of Ranmore church jutting from the surrounding woods, was dark against the blazing sky. The golden cockerel on the spire of Dorking church glittered against the vivid green of the

30

wooded slopes of Leith Hill. In the Holmsdale little copses and individual trees stood solid and distinct, sending long shadows across the burnished fields. Beyond White Down the line of the North Downs escarpment was clear-cut against the almost blinding light from the west. Distant Hindhead with its pylons, and Blackdown, were sharp and clear. That was indeed a view to remember.

There is another prospect to be seen from the top of Box Hill, less celebrated than that from the scarp crest though of scarcely less interest. It lies to the north. To see it one must go to the top of the river cliff, above the Whites. Because the long ridge of White Hill, above the Headley Valley, and the western side of the Mole gap converge to narrow the distant view it does not have the tremendous impact of that seen from the crest of the scarp. It is worth seeing however. On a clear day one can see right across the London Basin, past the wooded ridge at Esher and the gleam of light which marks the reservoirs at Staines, to the distant Chiltern Hills. If one goes to Juniper Top to see this view it enables one to look a little further round the corner of the Norbury slopes and so make out the massive outline of Windsor Castle on its little hill beside the Thames.

There are many other prospects of great beauty to be found on Box Hill. Every visitor to the place will have his or her favourite. Ours was that one sees on emerging from the woods on Lodge Hill, at the top of the steep slope into Juniper Bottom. The further slope of this little combe leads up to Juniper Top, beyond which the wooded ridges running down into the Headley Valley interlock, one behind the other, until they meet the distant sky-line where the little candle-snuffer shaped spire of Headley church is the only visible work of man in the scene. At all seasons of the year this is a view of delicate and colourful beauty: in spring when the white trunks of the small birches on the slope up to Juniper Top gleam amongst the soft green of their newly-opened leaves and the whitebeams seem almost incandescent against the rifleman-green of the yews: in summer, when the leaves are fully opened and the trees are solid masses of glistening green: in autumn, when the trunks of the birches become visible again amongst their thinning, yellowing leaves and the dogwood shows deeply crimson against the copper crowns of the beeches on the hill above the Ashurst Valley: in winter, when a dusting of snow on the ground throws into prominence the warm brown of the bare twigs on the birches, the rusty purple of the whitebeams and the grey boles of the beeches. Though more restricted in scope than the two great views from the top of Box Hill it surpasses them in charm and delicacy. It never fails to delight. However often one sees it one is always impatient to see it again, so much so in our case that, whatever part of Box Hill we intended to visit, more often than not our route to it lay this way.

CHAPTER THREE
THE MOLE AND ITS VALLEY

The Mole, in common with all the Wealden rivers, rises in the hills which form the central watershed of the High Weald. Being thickly wooded these hills are often termed the Forest Ridges. The head-waters of the Mole flow mostly from the western side of the Forest of Worth and the high ground which lies to the west of Crawley. The country here is remote and lonely, in places more reminiscent of the Pennines than the gentler landscapes of south-east England. Out-crops of the Tunbridge Wells sandstone form rampart-like edges which brood over the wooded valleys scooped by the streams out of the under-lying clays. It is a country of dense and secret woodlands, pheasant shoots, large isolated houses and ridge-top villages. Below these, in narrow, steep-sided valleys, run the rivers.

After leaving this high ground the Mole commences its serpentine course across the gently undulating country of the Weald Clay. Thus far it differs little in character from any of the Wealden rivers. Once the imposing gap, below Box Hill, by which the river traverses the North Downs and enters the London Basin, is reached however, the Mole assumes an individuality peculiar to itself, enshrined in legend and in the literature of our country. Here, so the old story goes, the Mole, like its animal namesake, disappears into the earth. There is no need to repeat here the many references from the works of writers in past centuries, to the Mole's supposed propensity to "snouzle underground". They are given in detail in Chapter 8. It is worth emphasising however that the exposure of this widely-held belief as a fallacy was due largely to the sharp and critical eye of Defoe.* He did what none of his predecessors (with the curious exception of John Evelyn, whose peculiar attachment to the legend of the dis-appearing Mole, even after he had visited the locality himself, remains unexplained) had done, namely, went to see for himself. In his trenchant demolition of the old legend he leaves us with no room to doubt that there is any such thing as a 'gulph' into which the river pours and that there is "No such thing as a river lost". He describes what does in fact take place, in a careful account on which it would be difficult to improve today. The river, he explains, loses

---

* Defoe is none too clear on the matter. In an earlier paragraph he does write of the river "working its way underground", but from what he states later it seems he means only that part of it which goes into the swallows.

water by reason of its disappearing down very small, pipe-like hollows, called swallows, in the chalk of its banks. In his own words they "diminish the stream much" but "do not swallow it up".

Today we know more about swallow-holes, which occur only in limestone rocks, of which chalk is a form. They result from the propensity of limestone to be dissolved by water. Swallow-holes of great size are found in the mountain limestone of northern Britain, some of them, such as Alum Pot and Gaping Ghyll, being nationally famous. In chalk, however, which is a much softer rock than limestone, swallow-holes never reach any great dimensions, for the loosened rock continually crumbles and fills them in. Defoe knew this, asserting that they were never above one-quarter of an inch in diameter, a fact confirmed by modern research. He also knew that there were many of them in the bed of the Mole where it traverses the chalk, again a fact well-known to geologists today. Even more to Defoe's credit is that he observed that the water lost down the swallows returned to the river as it approaches Leatherhead "in thousands of little springs".

All of Defoe's observations have been confirmed by modern investigators. Yet it is in the nature of mankind to relish a good story and be loth to relinquish it. On one of our earliest visits to Box Hill we were assured by a gentleman with whom we had got into conversation, that there were two rivers between Box Hill and Leatherhead, one above ground, the other following the same course, but underground. Camden might have nodded his head in approval, Defoe have shaken his in despairing disapproval.

As Defoe pointed out, the loss of water to the swallows diminishes the river. He would have been interested to know by how much. The average flow of the Mole above Burford Bridge is 63 million gallons a day. At Leatherhead it is 55 million gallons. Thus 8 million gallons have disappeared somewhere. Some of the loss is due to evaporation, some to seepage. But the amount lost in this manner cannot be as great as 8 million gallons a day. The major part of the loss must therefore be the water which goes down the swallows. There are known to be about 20 swallow-holes in the stretch of the river between Burford Bridge and Leatherhead. (The number varies as some become choked with alluvium and others form.) Below Leatherhead the flow averages about 98 million gallons a day. This increased flow is partly accounted for by water returning to the Mole from springs. 'Official figures'

34

The swallows are situated mainly in the banks where the river comes into direct contact with the chalk. Much of the bed of the river is insulated from the process of solution by the layer of alluvium which it has deposited there. It is not easy to detect the swallows as they are hidden below the surface of the water. Sometimes however one may perceive a gentle circulation of the water. Leaves and other debris rotate slowly around instead of drifting on with the current. In such places one may be fairly sure that there is a swallow-hole concealed beneath the surface.

Occasionally, in long-continued dry spells, when the volume of water coming down the Mole from the Weald is greatly diminished, the loss of water to the swallows may lower the level of the river to the point where it ceases to flow in the stretch through the meadows below Burford Bridge. When this happens the river becomes a chain of stagnant pools separated by stretches where one may walk dry-shod over its bare, flint-strewn bed. By looking around one may find places where these pools can be seen draining away in a thin trickle down one of the swallows. It provides a good opportunity to see how small these are. The river itself will not be found flowing again until near Leatherhead. Below the town it will be found flowing normally, fed by the springs to which reference has already been made.

Solution of the chalk produces features similar to swallow-holes, though often much larger, in the sides of the valley at some distance from the river. Occasionally the circumstances in which these are revealed can be alarming. The story of the tree which dropped vertically into a chasm behind a house in Mickleham in 1940 is well-known. The chasm appeared suddenly without any warning though subterranean rumblings heard during the previous night had given some indication that something out of the ordinary might be expected to happen. The tree, an oak of medium size, disappeared completely from view apart from some of its upper branches. These were visible for a time above the water which filled the hole to within fifteen feet of the surface of the ground. In places there are deep dells in the sides of the Mole valley which must have resulted from similar collapses of holes caused by solution of the chalk in the past. One of these dells lies behind the Weypole, to the left of the steep path which leads up the hill to Swiss Cottage. Smaller holes sometimes appear. They are circular and have vertical sides. One of these may still be seen in the field near Burford Bridge. It is within a yard or two of the river bank. When the roundabout opposite the Burford

Bridge Hotel was being constructed three of these solution hollows were revealed. It proved impractical to fill them in and they were covered with concrete umbrellas on which the road was laid.

The Mole bears along much sediment derived from the various clays and sandstones over which it flows in its upper course. This sediment makes its waters murky. They have not the clarity of the waters of the Darent which has no Wealden course and flows mainly on the chalk. It is not easy to spot fish in the Mole. Sometimes one may do so where the river is not very deep and the sun shines through the water from behind one. Yet while the river itself is not of a remarkable nor outstandingly beautiful character, the valley which it has cut through the four-miles-wide belt of the chalk, is. The river cliff, with its beech and yew woodland, interspersed with patches of bare chalk, is both beautiful and unique. The origin of this magnificent feature, explained in the previous chapter, provides impressive confirmation of the fact that running water is by far the most important agent in the creation of landscape. Standing on the edge of the river cliff, above the Whites, one perceives further evidence of this. The beautiful, steep-sided, wooded valley into which one looks is largely the work of the Mole, or rather, as described in the previous chapter, of the Mole's more powerful ancestors. It is unlikely that so small a stream as that which runs through the gap nowadays could have cut so large a valley. Cubic miles of countryside have been excavated and transported by the predecessors of the present river into the Thames which, in turn, has transported them into the sea.

In most years we managed to walk the length of the valley from Leatherhead at least once. It was a walk we usually reserved for mid-summer because of the refreshing coolness provided by the nearby river and the fact that so much of it lies beneath the shade of the trees which line the river's course and clothe its valley sides. It is not possible to follow the actual course of the river throughout as some of it lies in private grounds and some of it is physically inaccessible. This is no disadvantage however as one has the alternatives of the tree-shaded rides below Norbury Park or the paths through the farmlands which lie upon the valley floor.

After leaving Leatherhead one can follow the river throughout as far as Priory Farm. The path leads through pleasant meadows where skylarks sing overhead and many other little birds twitter and flit about in the hedgerows, linnets, goldfinches, greenfinches, titmice and flycatchers for example. However it is the water birds which one is most anxious to see. By taking one's time and proceeding quietly one has a good chance of seeing most of the birds which belong primarily to the river. Sometimes one has a moment of rare good fortune as on a memorable occasion when we saw two kingfishers and a Heron all at the same time. The kingfishers flew past in quick succession, vivid flashes of blue. The Heron was standing statuesque in the shallows beside the far bank. Despite our quiet approach and attempts to conceal ourselves behind the dense vegetation which borders the river at this point it had already seen us. One unblinking yellow eye was fixed upon us, the head held high on long, drawn-out neck. Then the bird spread broad wings on which it lifted itself up from the water, above the alders lining the bank and flapped away up river. The possibility of such moments as this made the walk by the river always an exciting one. It was a brief reminder of a simpler, more elemental past, when no distant growl of traffic, no airliner bellowing overhead, disturbed the peace of the Mole valley.

The Mole has its own distinctive bird life. Moorhens scuttle across the water, alarmed at one's approach. Often in summer a duck Mallard may be seen swimming past with her brood of ducklings close behind her. In recent years a new species of duck, the Mandarin, has colonised the Mole. The drake is an extremely handsome little bird, with a black head, white face and red bill. He is adorned with what look like orange-coloured side-whiskers and a pair of stiffly upstanding orange-coloured 'sails', like an airliner's tail fins, on his wings. The duck is a plain little grey bird. We once saw one, with her brood of tiny, newly-hatched ducklings, seeming little bigger than bumble bees, moving quietly through the thick vegetation on the river bank.

Of the birds which belong almost exclusively to the Mole valley the most delightful is the Grey Wagtail. Apart from the Kingfisher, which one sees much less frequently, no bird brings more life and gaiety to the river scene. One particular instance when we were made vividly aware of this remains fresh in our memories. We were walking by the Mole on one of those wonderful May evenings when there seems to be some special quality in the sunlight so that it confers an exceptional clarity of colour on everything on which it falls. The various different greens of the trees beside the river bank shone with a glow like that from a stained glass window against the massed woodland of the river cliff above them. The bare chalk patches of the Whites were tinged pink by the sun's rays. Underneath the trees on the river bank the sunlight fell in splashes of gold on the khaki-coloured waters of the Mole and its sandy banks. Overhanging branches were faithfully reflected in the deep pools away from the main current, each individual twig and leaf sharp and distinct, brilliant with light. In this sunlit river world two grey wagtails were flitting to and fro across the surface of the water, engaged in what seemed like some avian dance, part running, part flying. They would flutter across the river quite slowly, but with rapidly fanning wings, at times almost hovering, then alight on some piece of floating weed or driftwood where they would remain for a few seconds with gently pulsating tails. After this brief pause they would spring into the air again and repeat their dance across the river. It was a quite unforgettable sight. In that private, sunlit river world it was a rare picture of purest beauty.

We saw grey wagtails by the Mole every year until 1963. The severe winter of 1962-63 drastically reduced their numbers. We saw very few grey wagtails for, several years afterwards and had no certain evidence of their breeding there until 1971 when we saw two little parties of juveniles early in June.

In addition to the truly water birds of the Mole valley there are

Grey wagtail

several species which one sees there more frequently than in other parts of the Box Hill area, probably because the proximity of water is necessary to them. This applies particularly to the finches which are thirsty birds. Greenfinches for instance, always seem more numerous beside the Mole than elsewhere. We often saw bullfinches, goldfinches and yellowhammers near the river and it is only there in the Box Hill area that one is likely to find tree sparrows. In the winter siskins are sometimes to be seen in the trees beside the Mole. These little finches are particularly likely to be found in alders on the seeds of which they feed. The alder is a water-loving tree and numbers grow beside the river. In summer spotted flycatchers seemed to us more numerous near the Mole than elsewhere, no doubt attracted by the large numbers of insects always to be found beside water.

There are in places, shallows at the edge of the river to which come many birds to drink and bathe. It is always worthwhile to spend half an hour concealed near to one of these for there is nearly always something interesting to be seen. One will, in fact, see more birds in this way than in an hour or two of walking. At one such place, near Swanworth Farm, we once saw a Blue Tit, a Yellowhammer and a Grey Wagtail, a most colourful sight, all splashing in the shallow water together, while a Spotted Flycatcher hawked for insects over-head and swallows skimmed up and down the river. What more perfect way to spend a summer evening than lying in the shade, watching such a pretty sight, could possibly be imagined?

Swanworth Farm is the point at which one rejoins the river after leaving it at Priory Farm. Between the two farms the river runs through private ground. To avoid this one has a choice of two routes, both equally inviting. One can take the path through the fields, where swallows and house martins wheel overhead and turtle doves croon in the trees; or one can follow the rides beneath the magnificent beech trees on the slopes below Norbury Park. The latter route has the advantage of providing glimpses of the river which runs some way below at the foot of the steep slope below the track. In this way one has the chance of observing some of the water birds when they are peacefully unaware of one's presence, a family of mallards perhaps or a Moorhen pecking about with constantly jerking head, amongst the reeds. There are also the birds which live in the woods on these slopes, woodpeckers, tree creepers and nuthatches. In summer the songs of some of the warblers may be heard, Chiffchaff, Blackcap and occasionally, if one is very fortunate, a Wood Warbler.

The open grassy slopes which occur here and there amongst the woodland on the western side of the valley are notable for their wealth of wild flowers. We would look for and always find, in their seasons, marjoram, wild mignonette, eyebright, harebells, clustered bell-flower and the tall sulphur-coloured mullein, together with many other wild flowers of the chalk. Some of them, for instance thyme and rock-rose, seemed to grow to unusual size and be of particu-larly brilliant colouring on these slopes. In the shady woodland areas one can find such delightful flowers as woodruff, yellow archangels, herb paris, wood spurge and violet. Flowering shrubs, some of them peculiar to the chalk, wayfaring tree, elder, spindle and privet, also grow in these open stretches. One slightly disappointing aspect of this side of the Mole valley from the botanist's point of view is that few wild orchids appear to grow there. We could never satisfactorily account for this. However orchids are unpredictable plants. We often searched areas which seemed suitable for them without finding any.

Despite the rarity of these favourite chalkland flowers of ours the western side of the valley had an especial fascination for us. Its slopes are secluded and quite difficult of access. The best of the floral displays take a good deal of finding and are reached only by some quite arduous scrambling. There is one particular slope which has something of the air of mystery of a deserted garden. Big clumps of wild iris grow there along with meadowsweet and dropwort. Bushes of pink and white wild roses hang their scented sprays above them. Under the trees are drifts of the charming and charmingly named enchanter's nightshade. It is a magical place, quite different in character from Box Hill. Not far away is the stretch of woodland with the curious name of the Druid's Grove. It has the atmosphere of a place where much has happened in ages widely separated from our own. Today it is deserted and overgrown, the home of foxes and badgers. One meets few people there at any time, yet one has the feeling all the time of being watched. It is with a sense of relief that one looks across the valley to the familiar outline of Box Hill. The well-known prospect provides reassurance that one is not lost nor somehow strayed into the past. As the shadows fall and the evening air grows cool in these western woodlands the far side of the valley is flooded with light from the declining sun. In late summer one has then a glorious prospect of the richest colours, from the harvest yellows, strong and vigorous, of the fields on the far hillside, beyond the valley, to the dark greens of the tree which line the Mole.

These trees of the Mole valley demand a special panegyric all to themselves. There can be few places near to London where trees grow to such size and magnificence. This applies equally to the beeches and yews of the valley sides and the limes and elms, horse chestnuts and oaks, of the farmlands beside the Mole. There is a grove of limes by the path to Lodge Farm which must be amongst the tallest in south-eastern England. We once saw a Robin singing from the very top of one of them, a place which one would not have expected any bird other than a Mistle Thrush to use as a song-post. There are also some magnificent trees around Fredley and in the dip below Juniper Hall, where the Headley Valley runs down to the Mole.

On leaving the slopes of Norbury or the meadows by Cowslip Bank and Swanworth Farm one has the choice of two routes back to Box Hill station. One is the field path past Lodge Farm which leads by a bridge over the Mole to the path by Cowslip Farm and then beside the railway line. The other follows the track above Ham Bank from which one descends by a steep slope to the path through the copse called Nicol's Field. Both routes have their attractions. On the whole we preferred the latter as it maintains contact with the river until one reaches the railway nearly at the end of the walk. This final stretch beside the Mole has particular charm because of the fine display of yellow water-lilies which appears upon it in mid-summer. Another yellow flower which blooms around the same time in this part of the Mole valley is the small balsam. Further up the river, near Burford Bridge, its Asiatic relative, the Himalayan balsam, a foreign invader, now common on Britain's rivers, grows in rich profusion.

Approaching Box Hill station from down-river, the last stage of the walk is beside the railway embankment, the sides of which are always rich with wild flowers. Ox-eye daisies, cowslips, buttercups, pink and white campion, speedwell, bugle, knapweed, jack-by-the-hedge and greater celandine are some of the many wild flowers which grow here in profusion. There is a stout wire fence at the foot of the embankment which makes access to it impossible. Protected in this way the wild flowers are safe from the hands of those thoughtless folk who must pick everything they see, and thus remain a delight to us all.

It was late in the evening as a rule when we reached this final stage of the walk by the Mole. In the trees below Foxbury the rooks would be cawing sleepily at their nests. Perhaps a late Cuckoo would call from the woods higher up the valley side or maybe we would hear the eerie yelping of a Little Owl from the farmlands down the river. Often dusk would have fallen before we reached West Humble and we would finish our walk by moon or starlight. The looming towers of the elms in the meadows and the tree-clad ridge of the slope behind Foxbury would be black as Indian ink against the electric blue of the night sky, the only sounds the swishing of our footsteps in the dew-drenched grass, the munching of the cattle feeding in the fields and the calling of the tawny owls in the woods around Norbury. At last we would reach the narrow path which leads to the final stile into West Humble Lane and the welcoming glow of the lights framing the Stepping Stones Inn. Yet, even as we made our way there, to rest tired limbs and refresh ourselves before our train left for home and bed, our eyes would be on the familiar shape of Box Hill, dimly seen in the night sky, and our thoughts be with the Mole, slipping dark and silent through its tunnel of trees at the foot of the Whites, on its way to Leatherhead, by the way we had come.

CHAPTER FOUR
THE BIRD LIFE OF BOX HILL

In the comparatively small area of which Box Hill is the centre there is considerable variety of differing natural habitats, ranging from the open, grassy slopes of the escarpment, where numbers of people congregate at week-ends and holiday times, to quite extensive and largely unfrequented stretches of scrub and woodland. There are also the contrasting habitats of the Mole valley and Headley Heath not far away. Consequently the bird life of the whole locality, including the two last-named habitats, is varied and the number of species one could expect to see sufficient to satisfy all but those who do not consider a day's bird-watching a success unless they have seen at least two or three rarities. Anyone making regular visits to the area over a period should eventually record between 80 and 90 species of birds. Our own total, achieved in visits made over a period of 20 years, was 92 species. A few of these have now disappeared from the Box Hill locality so it is unlikely that our total will be exceeded in the immediate future, but it provides a target at which to aim.

All the common birds of the English countryside occur on Box Hill, the blackbirds, thrushes, robins, wrens, dunnocks, titmice and finches. The corvine tribe is common. There is a rookery in the trees beside the Mickleham Road, just below the steep slope at the rear of Box Hill. Jackdaws nest in the woods. Carrion crows and magpies range over the whole area. The Jay is not so frequently seen but is widespread in the woodlands. Wood pigeons are numerous, nesting in all the woodlands and feeding in small parties on the open grassy areas. Swallows nest in the outbuildings of farms, house martins under the eaves of farms and dwelling houses wherever they are permitted to do so. Swifts may be seen feeding overhead during the summer months though they probably nest no nearer than Dorking. There was a colony of sand martins in an old quarry in Dorking, explaining why one sometimes saw these birds feeding over the Mole and occasionally above Box Hill itself.

The open areas of chalk grassland, such as the scarp face of Box Hill and Juniper Top, are used as feeding grounds by parties of rooks, jackdaws, starlings, wood pigeons and mistle thrushes. Individual birds which may sometimes be seen there include green woodpeckers and magpies. Until the severe winter of 1962-63 wiped them out, woodlarks used to nest on at least one of these open areas. The only bird likely to be found nesting there now is an occasional Tree Pipit.

The loss of the Woodlark is perhaps the saddest Box Hill has suffered where birds are concerned. Its song has an ethereal quality unique amongst those of British birds. Some people consider it superior even to that of the Nightingale, though it is not so powerful. Like the Skylark the Woodlark usually sings on the wing, not in vertical ascent, as the Skylark does, but in level flight, on a roughly circular path, a little above tree-top height. To hear one, as we often did, before 1963, singing as it circled above Juniper Top, was an experience of sheer delight.

The richest in bird life of the various habitats on Box Hill are the little combes which run northwards at the back of the hill. These contain a variety of low-growing shrubs and small trees in which bramble, whitebeam, wayfaring tree, elder, birch, dogwood and gorse predominate. In some cases the sides of the combes are thickly wooded, beech and yew being the chief trees. The two eastern combes contain a lot of bracken. This mixture of various types of cover; with the rich insect life found there, provides a habitat attractive to considerable numbers of birds and so to the bird-watcher. Small birds are numerous — robins, dunnocks, wrens, blackbirds, thrushes, the various titmice — Great, Blue, Coal, Marsh and Long-tailed — bullfinches, chaffinches, greenfinches, goldfinches, linnets, yellowhammers and occasionally redpolls. These are residents which remain throughout the year. In summer their numbers are increased by the arrival of a number of migrants. Chief amongst these are the warblers. Five of our British warblers — Blackcap, Garden Warbler, Willow Warbler, Chiffchaff and Whitethroat — will usually be found in these combes. The rarer Grasshopper Warbler and Lesser Whitethroat have been recorded there also.

One of the most numerous of the warblers in the combes used to be the Whitethroat. It is less common nowadays, for a variety of reasons, but a few may still be found. Whitethroats are inquisitive little birds. If you are patient, sooner or later one will pop up on some vantage point such as the top of a gorse bush, so it can have a look at you. Then you may note its grey head, chestnut-brown back and the pure white of the throat from which it gets its name. The squeaky, chattering little song is an infallible indication of the bird's presence. It is sometimes uttered from the interior of a bush or

44

thicket, sometimes on the wing, the bird fluttering upwards in jerky, dancing flight, rattling out its song as it does so.

The other warblers are less easy to see and one has to depend a good deal on knowing their songs to identify them. The Chiffchaff is the easiest to recognise because of the double note "tip-tap-tip-tap-tip-tap" from which it gets its name. This is particularly useful in the case of the Chiffchaff as it is virtually indistinguishable in the field from its close relative the Willow Warbler. Their songs are entirely different however. That of the Willow Warbler is a sweet and gentle warble, seeming to diminish in volume as it proceeds. Though brief it is a complete phrase. As it utters its song every minute or two in spring one soon becomes familiar with it.

The other two warblers which will always be found in the combes are the Blackcap and the Garden Warbler. They occur in other places of course. The Blackcap and the Chiffchaff are likely to turn up in almost any locality where there are plenty of trees. One is fairly sure to hear one or both of these warblers in such places as Ashurst Rough, the woodlands around Norbury, even the gardens of Mickleham and West Humble. The Garden Warbler is less far-ranging though the woodlands on the top of Box Hill usually contain one or two pairs. It is most likely to be found in the combes however.

Blackcap and Garden Warbler are easy to distinguish in the field. The former is a silvery-grey bird with a brownish-grey back and conspicuous black cap, from which it gets its name. In the female bird the cap is bright brown. The Garden Warbler is a rather bulkier bird than most of the warblers. It is uniformly dull brown apart from the greyish-white underparts, giving the impression of a plumper bird than the Blackcap. Neither is very easy to see and the song is the best means of identification. That of the Garden Warbler is a rich and melodious, rather hurried warble, which ripples on without a break, for several seconds at a time. The Blackcap's song is even more beautiful. It is of a more finished quality and less hurried, delivered in quite brief phrases, separated by short periods of silence. One of the most beautiful of British bird songs, it has a joyousness which makes it always a delight to hear. On some bright day in May, when the breeze ruffles the young green leaves so that their silvery undersides flash and twinkle in the sunlight; when the bluebells are drifts of azure in the shadier depths of the woods and their fragrance is borne to you along with that mysterious, indescribable scent which comes from growing things, there comes from this green world a sudden snatch of rippling, lilting bird-song. It is as if the glinting leaves and shining blossoms had themselves burst into music. The song of the Blackcap, thus heard, belongs to May, the time of hawthorn in bloom and tall plumes on the horse chestnut trees, as the Willow Warbler's song belongs to April, the time of faint green in the shaws, above the primroses and cowslips.

Britain's foremost songster, the Nightingale, is, unfortunately, a rarity on Box Hill. One must go to Bookham or Holmwood Commons to be sure of hearing one, though they have been recorded from the thickets at the foot of the escarpment. On the rare occasions when a Nightingale has been heard on Box Hill it has almost always been in one of the combes, so, for the optimist, these are the most likely places in which to listen for an hour or two on some warm May evening, in the hope of hearing one.

Another bird of the dusk, the Nightjar, used to be heard on summer nights, uttering its peculiar reeling song from the scrub on the upper slopes of the combes. They have not been recorded there for some years but may still be found on Headley Heath. The Woodcock, an interesting and rather mysterious bird, which, like the Nightjar, haunts the twilight hour, still occurs, in very small numbers, in the scrub in summer. It is most likely to be seen on its nuptial flight. Known as "roding", it is the male bird's display flight. It follows a circular path at tree-top height. Those with keen hearing will hear the bird utter a queer little grunting cry or sometimes a soft "chisick", like a Pied Wagtail's call, as it passes overhead.

The handsome Red-backed Shrike, which used to be found in the combes in summer, has not been seen there for some years. Its numbers have decreased drastically in recent years. Barely thirty years ago it bred as near to London as Mitcham Common.

Tree pipits are sometimes to be seen and heard song-flighting from one of the taller trees in the combes. Their chief haunt near Box Hill however is Headley Heath, where they are found in company with their close relative the Meadow Pipit.

Two birds which do not sing in the conventional sense but whose voices are pleasant to hear in summertime, the Cuckoo and the Turtle Dove, may be found anywhere on Box Hill except on the open grassy areas and in the denser parts of the woodlands. The combes are the most likely places in which to look for them however. The Cuckoo has become less numerous on Box Hill in the last twenty years or so but the Turtle Dove seems to be maintaining its status as a fairly common summer visitor. One may be glad about this as its purring coo is a pleasant addition to the summer chorus of bird song on Box Hill.

The woodland areas of Box Hill lack the great variety of bird life to be found in the combes. They can indeed be surprisingly birdless in places and one might walk for a mile or more without seeing very much of note. Nevertheless they are worth searching, being the home of the truly arboreal birds, Nuthatch, Tree Creeper and the woodpeckers. In the dense tree cover none of these is easily seen and it is advisable to proceed slowly and quietly, keeping a sharp look-out, to have much chance of seeing one of them. The Tree Creeper is perhaps the most likely to be spotted as it is not a particularly shy bird. It is however, a small one and it is often a matter of luck whether one sees one or not. Its habit of flitting from one tree to another and creeping rapidly up their trunks in a series of little jerky movements, makes it easy to identify. The Nuthatch is not a shy bird either. It is common throughout the Box Hill area wherever there are tall trees. In spring its high, clear whistle and long trill are familiar sounds in the woodlands. The Nuthatch is the only one of the arboreal birds which runs down the tree trunks as well as up them. It is a handsome bird, with its slate-grey back, warm chestnut underparts and black streak through the eye.

Our two common woodpeckers, Green and Great Spotted, are widely distributed in the woodlands. Of the two the Green is the more likely to be seen because of its habit of visiting the open areas, such as Juniper Top, in search of ants on which it feeds. It is a wary bird and takes flight at once if disturbed. When it does so its large size, green colouring and distinctive flight, a series of shallow, undulating swoops, make it easy to identify. So too does its weird cry, like a peal of mocking laughter, from which it gets its old English name of Yaffle.

The Great Spotted Woodpecker, despite its size and striking black and white plumage, is less likely to be seen for it is a shy and somewhat furtive bird. One is more likely to hear the drum-roll of the male, sounding from some dead branch in early spring, or the anxious "quit" call of the parents if one happens to approach the tree in which the nest hole is located, than to see the bird itself.

The Lesser Spotted or Barred Woodpecker is uncommon in the Box Hill woodlands. It does occur however and is probably quite often overlooked. Not only is it a small bird, about the size of a Great

Great spotted woodpecker

Tit, but it spends most of its time in the tree tops where it is extremely difficult to see. The best time to look out for it is in spring when it draws attention to its presence by its call, a high-pitched "kee-kee-kee", not unlike the cry of a Kestrel.

Another uncommon bird of the woodlands, whose furtive habits make it extremely difficult to see, is the Hawfinch. It does occur in the Box Hill woods but, like the Lesser Spotted Woodpecker, is frequently overlooked because of its similar habit of confining itself to the tree tops. Nor does it have an easily recognised call which further diminishes one's prospects of recording it.

Just as wary as the Hawfinch but much more common in the woodlands is the Jay. Its presence is most often revealed by the harsh, screeching cry, a clear indication that, while you may not have seen the bird, it has certainly seen you and is letting the rest of the inhabitants of the woodland know. If the Jay's screaming is some distance away however the chances are that it has seen something else of whose presence it disapproves, possibly a prowling fox or stoat, but most likely an owl. The Brown or Tawny Owl is common all over Box Hill in the woods. Sometimes one will disturb one from its daytime roosting site and can then enjoy the sight of the big brown bird, wafting away on soundless wings, through the trees.

Four members of the warbler family already mentioned, Blackcap, Garden Warbler, Willow Warbler and Chiffchaff, all occur in the Box Hill woodlands, though usually in, or near an open glade. A fifth, the Wood Warbler, is, as its name suggests, strictly a woodland bird. It used to be found on Box Hill, where we had proof that it nested, but in our experience, is so no longer. Occasionally one would appear in spring and sing for a day or two but these birds never stayed. It is a pity if the Wood Warbler has disappeared from the Box Hill woodlands, for it is one of the most delightful of our summer visitors. Seen at close quarters, flitting about in the beech leaves, it is an exquisite little bird, more brightly green and yellow than the Chiffchaff or Willow Warbler and very dainty in its movements. The slow, moth-like flight, performed as part of its mating display, is an entrancing sight. Its song is unmistakable, a long, sibilant twitter, uttered with rapidly quivering wings, followed by a long, drawn-out flute-like note, several times repeated, often as the bird descends from a higher to a lower branch with the moth-like flight already referred to. W.H. Hudson described its song as the true voice of the beech-woods, "the woodland sound that is like no other". Box Hill is the poorer for its loss.

While wood pigeons inhabit all the Box Hill woodlands, stock doves seem to have a preference for certain parts of them, notably the beech hanger opposite Juniper Hall and the woods on the Whites, above the Mole. Their peculiar deep, crooning note is distinctive and makes them easy to identify without seeing the birds. They are hole nesters so availability of suitable nesting sites may influence their distribution. Other birds which nest in holes, chiefly jackdaws and starlings, are common in the Box Hill woods. This must result in considerable competition for the limited number of such nest sites available and possibly be to the detriment of the less aggressive species such as the Stock Dove.

Winter, when the trees are bare, is the best time to see the resident birds of the woodlands. It is always a delightful experience, on some bright winter day, to come upon a little flock of noisy, lively titmice, working its way through the trees. These flocks often include members of all the titmice commonly to be found on Box Hill, Great, Blue, Coal, Marsh and Long-tailed. Sometimes they are accompanied by goldcrests and even tree creepers and nuthatches. No doubt the reasons for these associations are availability of food and mutual protection from predators but one often has the impression that the birds enjoy each others' company.

One also finds flocks of chaffinches, sometimes accompanied by bramblings, in the woods during the winter. In this case availability of food supply in the form of beechmast undoubtedly brings these two closely related species into association with one another. A mixed flock of chaffinches and bramblings is always a pretty sight, the black and white wing marking of both species, the pink breasts of the cock chaffinches, the salmon-pink shoulder patches and white rumps of the bramblings conspicuous against the rich brown carpet of the fallen beech leaves through which they are moving.

The small wooded areas in which yew trees predominate, found on the sides of the western combes, do not usually hold many birds. Goldcrests regularly frequent them. Less often one will find coal tits, chaffinches and robins there. In winter the yew berries provide a supply of food and the trees themselves good shelter for numbers of song thrushes and redwings, sometimes with fieldfares. The latter two species are migrants which come to Britain from northern Europe in the winter. The Redwing may be distinguished from other thrushes by its conspicuous cream-coloured eye-stripe and the rusty red on the flanks, seen best in flight, from which it gets its name. The Fieldfare is a larger bird and much more wary. Its grey head, dark chestnut back, black tail and heavily streaked breast make it easy to identify. In flight the pale grey of the lower back is distinctive, as is the strong call-note, a sharp "chack-chack".

Spotted flycatchers are common in summer in almost all places where there are trees on Box Hill, from the banks of the Mole to the woodland around the cafés on the top of the hill. The Flycatcher is a brown bird with a whitish, streaked breast. It is a silent bird and such notes as it utters are so quiet as to be audible only to those with keen hearing. Its manner of catching its prey by darting out from some vantage point and snapping it in mid-air, make it easy to recognise.

Pied wagtails occur in many parts of Box Hill. They are just as likely to be seen trotting about on the road which runs along the top of the hill as in the meadows by the Mole. The term Water Wagtail is something of a misnomer. The Grey Wagtail, on the other hand, is unlikely to be seen far from the river.

The last to be considered of the various habitats in the Box Hill area, Headley Heath, has its own characteristic bird associations. This is the chief haunt of the Skylark in the locality. Its song may be heard there from early in the year until late in the summer. The Meadow and Tree Pipit are also always to be found on the Heath. The former is rarely seen elsewhere in the area but the latter sometimes occurs away from the Heath, usually where trees adjoin open grass sward, as on the scarp face or the sides of some of the combes. The two pipits are almost indistinguishable in the field but can easily be identfied from the difference in their songs and the manner in which they are delivered. The Meadow Pipit flies up into the air from the ground for some twenty feet, then descends slowly, with outspread wings and tail, singing as it does so. The song is a simple and not very strong repetition of the note which gives it its name, a reedy "tsip-tsip". The Tree Pipit has the same manner of flying up into the air, then floating slowly down, singing as it does so, but the ascent is usually made from a tree rather than the ground. Furthermore the song is stronger and more accomplished than that of the Meadow Pipit. It is completed by several long, drawn-out notes, "dwee-dwee-dwee" far-carrying and of particular sweetness of tone. Quite often a Tree Pipit will sing from a stationary perch on a tree or bush but sooner or later it will fly upwards and sing in the manner described. Tree pipits are migrants and so occur only in summer. The Meadow Pipit is resident and so is likely to be found on Box Hill at any time of the year.

The Stonechat and the Whinchat have both been recorded on

Headley Heath in time gone by. The Whinchat seems to have deserted the locality completely. The Stonechat, a bird which has been increasing in numbers in southern counties recently, is to be found on several Surrey heaths and there seems no reason why Headley Heath should not be among them.* It is an attractive and conspicuous little bird, with its black head, white collar and rusty-red breast, easy to identify.

Many other birds which are found in other parts of the Box Hill area may also be seen or heard on Headley Heath, making it a place of sheer delight for the bird-watcher to roam over in spring and summer. There, in May, the Cuckoo does indeed "call all day". On warm summer nights the Nightjar may still be heard, reeling from some convenient branch. Green woodpeckers are sometimes found there, far from woodland, doubtless feeding on the ants which are common in this sandy environment. Kestrels hover overhead. Carrion crows range over the Heath, unwelcome visitors, preying on small nestlings, an unpleasant activity in which they are often joined by magpies and jays. Swallows, house martins and swifts sweep back and forth over the heather and gorse, collecting food for their nestlings. Yellowhammers and linnets are common. The sulphur-yellow and rich brown plumage of the cock Yellowhammer, together with its familiar song, make it an easy bird to recognise. Willow warblers are fairly numerous in most parts of the Heath in summer. The other warblers are less likely to be found there, though at one time whitethroats were common on Headley Heath.

Of the raptorial birds, falcons, hawks and owls, only the Kestrel and Tawny Owl are at all common in the Box Hill area. Tawny owls inhabit all the wooded parts of Box Hill. On still summer evenings their melodious calls can be heard from far and near. Kestrels appear to breed mainly outside the area, though visiting it regularly in search of prey. The Sparrow Hawk is uncommon. However its wariness and manner of hunting make it much less likely to be seen than the Kestrel. While the Kestrel hovers overhead, eyeing the ground for prey, on which it pounces, the Sparrow Hawk depends on surprise, hurtling suddenly low over the tree tops, or dashing at speed down one of the combes or along one of the rides in the woodland, to strike down any small bird unfortunate enough to be caught in the open. The Hobby, which breeds in one or two places in Surrey, very occasionally visits the Box Hill area on hunting expeditions.

* Since this chapter was written, breeding has been proved on the Heath.

52

The Little Owl prefers more open country than the Tawny Owl. Thus it is more likely to be found in the farmlands which surround Box Hill than on the hill itself. The Barn Owl, which has been recorded on Box Hill in the past, is probably to be found there no longer.

Partridges occasionally occur on Box Hill, usually in one of the combes, to which they have strayed from the adjoining farmlands. The only other game bird present in the area is the Pheasant, which is resident in small numbers in the woods and the thickets in the combes. The absence of ponds and streams prohibits the presence in the area of water birds. One must go to the valley of the Mole, Leatherhead Ponds or Bury Hill Lake near Dorking and the ponds in the valley of the Pipp Brook between Westcott and Wotton for these.

Box Hill is thus a place mainly for the smaller birds. It is not a place where one is likely to record many rarities. There are days, particularly in winter, when one may not see many birds at all. The survey given here is a composite one, based on the observations of over twenty years. It might be compared to one of those nature trails where the list of what you might see can differ considerably from that of what you do see. At the end of such trails there will often be found disappointed people, complaining that the badger or the Nightjar, or some other beast, bird or insect which constituted the highlight of the trail, had failed to appear or to sing on cue. So it could easily appear to the more eager or impatient reader of this chapter. He or she may gain an impression of a richness of bird-life on Box Hill which is misleading. It is so often a matter of "jam tomorrow and jam yesterday but never jam today". Visit Box Hill often enough and you may well see as many birds there as we did. Visit it on a single day in spring or early summer and fifty will be a good score. In winter you will do well to exceed thirty. But it is not really the list that matters. It is the delight of bird-watching in a beautiful place, where the birds are wild and free, unharmed by man, that matters.

CHAPTER FIVE
THE WILD FLOWERS OF BOX HILL

Early memories of the Surrey Downs are of steep springy scarps and slopes down which it was a delight to roll and slide, and up which one could stride with an almost trampoline energy. There was something youthful in the way the grass and matted clover and the daisy rosettes sprang up again once the foot had moved on, or the rolling body had passed that way. Coming to a stop at the foot of a slope to find oneself regarding at point-blank range the tiny flower of purging flax, or one's nose pressed into a bank of thyme, or one's cheek in contact with the spines of stemless thistle, was a bitter-sweet delight that stayed with one from childhood days. Grown men and women, even folk in their late seventies, could confidently and steadily pace their grassy way up the uniformly graded slope from Meredith's House to the summit of Box Hill, and arrive at the full height of 625 feet above sea-level, scarcely panting and feeling years younger, to scan the view of the whole Weald from Salomon's Memorial, having conquered a hill long after they thought their hill-climbing days were over! All the way through life could be enjoyed the pleasures of the chalk sward.

Yet these slopes have not always been such a springboard, nor, if conditions change, will they remain so. Chalk sward is in a highly artificial state of equilibrium in the progression of natural vegetation; it passes from naked rock via lichens and mosses to sward, and then moves on via thorn-scrub towards the forest climax of yew or beech. The green lawns of Juniper Top are the result of many centuries of man's intervention. If one omits natural phenomena like weathering and leaching, the three most potent causes of the temporary victory of sward are trampling by man and his beasts of burden, grazing by cattle, pigs, goats, deer and particularly sheep; and most important of all, constant nibbling by thousands of rabbits. If any one of these factors is either removed or becomes dominant, then the balance is changed — either back towards bare rock, or on towards forest.

Too much trampling can cause denudation and desert conditions. The summit ridge from the Fort Café along the edge of the Mole Gap cliff running NNW down to the Burford Bridge Hotel looks sometimes as if it had an off-white snow cornice. It has been so trampled on and so wind-swept that the surface is bare chalk. Nothing can grow there at all. Too much grazing by pigs can produce the same effect. Hungry pigs root up all vegetation except the most poisonous plants like houndstongue and henbane. Only the guardianship of the National Trust has saved parts of Box Hill from the pig-wildernesses that have afflicted parts of the Chilterns and Kent Downs. Sheep are fairly omnivorous, but they crop short, without rooting up: they tend to encourage a vegetation that lies close to the ground. Horses and cattle are more selective. You have the chance of finding rare flowers like green-veined orchids even among grazing cattle, but you would not find them where sheep had recently grazed. People keep goats to eat the bramble shoots, but goats only resort to brambles when all other food supply fails. Then there is, or rather was, the rabbit!

Our period of observation on Box Hill embraced the pre-myxomatosis periods, as well as the years when blind and paralysed rabbits, suffering from this man-induced disease, filled the lanes and by-roads of England in 1953-4. The temporary removal of the rabbit demonstrated, as nothing else had done so clearly before, the truth that the chalk sward had no permanence. Rabbits themselves had been one of man's introductions in historic times, and rabbits graze almost as thoroughly as sheep. You have only to watch rabbits loose in a garden to see them ambling from asparagus to spring greens and on to rare flowers or noxious weeds, like children sampling a box of chocolates. What they eat first is immaterial — the box will be emptied! Rabbits and sheep for centuries kept down the young hawthorn and dogwood scrub before they could get a stranglehold. Rabbits and sheep encouraged those plants with low-growing and quick-flowering habits — sheep's fescue grass rather than the taller brome, daisies rather than the taller wild flowers.

Suddenly, in 1953, the rabbit was for the moment eliminated.

Knocking out a link in the chain can sometimes have surprising results. Soon the taller species of grass began to oust the shorter; small hawthorn seedlings began to rear their heads and dogwood and bramble shoots, above or below ground, began to spread. For a couple of years there was a splendid profusion of the taller wild flowers — yellow rattle, fragrant orchids, clustered bellflower — where few had been seen in previous summers. Then the clear sward of Juniper Top and the whole ridge from Headley Lane running up S.E., to the point where the birches, oaks and beeches of Ashurst Rough encroach, was confronted by an advancing line of dogwood scrub: the areas where woodlarks were once in the habit of pecking around for grass seed grew visibly narrower.

Fortunately for lovers of the chalk sward, Juniper Hall is a Field Centre where studies of these habitats are part of the courses organised there. It became obvious that as man had interfered by eliminating the rabbit, he must intervene again, or the dogwood scrub would become impenetrable to any walker not armed with a bill-hook! In a similar chalkland area, the Chiltern Hills, the problem was tackled by the Nature Conservancy in the Beacon Hill Reserve at Aston Rowant, by the experimental introduction of sheep. The National Trust then owned no sheep in the Box Hill area. Fortunately help was at hand in another form, the fund of energy and goodwill supplied by the Youth Movements and encouraged by the wardens of Juniper Hall. The Council for Nature Conservation Corps cleared the dogwood scrub, or, to give it its Latin name, "thelycrania sanguinea", with axe, matchet and bonfire. The chalk sward could breathe again, while in the artificial clearings orchids and bugle and self-heal and birdsfoot trefoil and blue fleabane could grow. The north-east slopes of Juniper Top might be losing their woodlarks and nightjars, but there was a profusion of fragrant orchids not seen for years.

The students of Juniper Hall have carried out some interesting experiments in plant ecology which are described in "Chalkland Ecology", written by John Sankey, recently Warden, and published by Heinemann Educational in 1966. A sample area of little trampled chalk sward and a similar one of heavily trampled were marked out and investigated in detail. Sheep's fescue grass flourished whether it was trampled or not, and so did ribwort. Hoary plantain and daisy seemed positively to relish trampling, but all the other plants did less well on footpaths than on less disturbed chalk sward. Bulbous buttercup, burnet saxifrage, purging flax, glaucous sedge, rough hawkbit, salad burnet, thyme and even stemless thistle showed these adverse reactions.

Thus a delicate balance is needed to maintain the short grass and numerous flowering plants — not too many walkers and not too few, not too many pony-trekkers, not too many sheep nor rabbits, yet not too few, and you have the paradise which John Gilmour and Max Walters in their book in Collins' New Naturalist Series, "Wild Flowers" and T.E. Lousley in his book on "Wild Flowers of the Chalk and Limestone" in the same series both eulogise. Box Hill is fortu-

nate in being the object of study by such botanists as these and in being under the intelligent management of the National Trust. Nor is chalk sward the only habitat that needs careful management on Box Hill. Areas of beech, yew and box, juniper and dogwood need careful limitation, encouragement and management according to plan if the wide variety of flowering plant species is to continue to flourish.

The flowers of the chalk sward form a balanced plant community. On Box Hill you can find species that are at the northern or western limits of their distribution; you can find specialist species which can grow only on soil with a large calcium carbonate content (these plants are termed calcicoles); you can find plants that adapt themselves either to lime or acid soils, but what you do not find are the plants that hate lime (the calcifuges). You find plants that dislike shade. You find plants with a built-in resistance to drought. Each species has its special character, but it is noteworthy how many of the wildflowers of the Box Hill sward reappear on the chalk of the South Downs or Chilterns or on the limestones of Britain and Europe. They are old friends whether you meet them in the chalklands of Normandy or the Durness limestone of Sutherland, the limestone pavements of Ingleborough or the Burren, the cliffs of the Dolomites or the Swabian Alps.

Some flowers will be in bloom between February and November, but even in the three winter months the botanist will find plants to excite him. Many species do indeed preserve their perennial energies by dying down completely beneath the surface in the winter, but there is a surprising number on the sward that do no such thing. The Juniper Hall students on 14 March 1962 recognised the leaves above the surface in a given area of the following species: bee orchid, bulbous buttercup, carline thistle, chalk milkwort, common milkwort, rock-rose, daisy, thyme, glaucous sedge, hairy violet, hoary plantain, mouse-ear hawkweed, pink centaury, ploughman's spikenard, rest-harrow, ribwort, salad burnet, sheep's fescue grass, small scabious, squinancywort and wild strawberry. There is green in the sward in the depths of winter as well as in the driest summer. Some features of the chalkland vegetation have special survival value. Hoary plantain, stemless thistle, carline thistle and mouse-ear hawkweed have developed the rosette habit, with leaves close to the ground: this eliminates competition, provides shelter against the desiccating effects of the east wind, and employs as large an area as possible for photosynthesis.* Birdsfoot trefoil, horseshoe vetch and black medick have developed a similar device, that of matting, which confers similar benefits for survival. In summer too chalk grass is greener than grass elsewhere. Other specialist devices give survival value. Mechanism to counter water loss is necessary on the porous chalk soils. On the dry August slopes of the Box Hill scarp something special is needed. Narrow leaves which roll under to avoid the sun is the ploy of sheep's fescue; long roots penetrating to the underlying rock are developed by the stemless thistle, salad burnet and small scabious. Excessive hairiness, as in hairy hawkbit, and tubers to store moisture underground (as with some orchids) are other examples of these specialist mechanisms for resisting drought.

But the main attraction of chalk flowers is not gracefulness of shape nor greenness of leaf, nor fragrance of scent. It is the wonderful variation and range of colour of the flowers themselves. To consider for a moment only those flowers on Box Hill which grow out on the open sward, there is the cream of the autumn ladies' tresses, the pinky-white of purging flax, dropwort, candytuft, squinancywort and most of the umbellifers, the golden yellow of the rock-rose and the orange-tinted yellows of the trefoils. Milkworts give you every hue from purple via deep blue to white. Bluer still are the speedwells, and then there is the sudden shock of the deep colour of viper's bugloss; there are the mauves of thyme and marjoram and the purples of clustered bellflower and felwort, to name but a few. The only colour missing from the chalk flora of Box Hill — and there seems to be a progression from green via yellow to blue, white and purple as the season advances — is the bright scarlet of the poppy or the scarlet pimpernel.

We knew that flowers which grew under the beech canopy could manage to attract insects and yet have green petals before the leaves of the beech trees came out. Hence dog's mercury and stinking hellebore and herb paris have green flowers very early in the year. But it never occurred to us that there was a possible explanation for this absence of scarlet from the chalk sward until we learnt that honey bees were colour blind so far as red is concerned. The colours of flowers are only incidentally to delight the eyes of Adam in the Garden of Eden or William Wordsworth by Ullswater — they aid in the process of procreation. Flowers which rely on bees for aiding pollination and cross-fertilisation can scarcely be red. The bees'

* See page 76

spectrum extends to ultra-violet, which is only detectable to the human eye in the laboratory. A red flower with no ultra-violet in its petals would be ignored by a bee and pollinated only by butterflies and insects which can perceive red. Heathers and thyme probably appear blue to a bee, as blue is a colour in the bees' spectrum. On the other hand bees can see a whole range of ultra-violets which the human eye misses — Karl von Frisch has said "Anyone who thinks the whole floral splendour of the earth was created to delight the eye of man should study the colour sense of the bees and the quality of the flowers' blossom and he will learn modesty!"†

Flowers, whatever colour they may appear to the individual observer, give great pleasure. Flowers, unlike birds, cannot fly away or even skulk, though the successful use of camouflage by orchids like the fly and musk is almost as remarkable as these same species' use of shape and scent as advertisement to insects! You could rely on finding the same series of flower species each year in the same places, though not always in the same numbers. We located the same species* year after year, some of them on the chalk sward, some of them by the wayside, some among scrub and under the beech canopy. We made a series of pilgrimages, of which more in a minute, to ensure that the rarer species were still there, but by and large one could rely on finding the flowers at the right dates in a way no ornithologist locating a bird species could rival. The clump of cerastium arvensis bloomed on Juniper Top each year; the woodlarks frequented the same area only intermittently. A late frost might hold the season back, but there could be no such disasters as the sward on the South Downs sometimes suffered from the blown salt in a spring storm along the Channel coast. Exceptional winters like that of 1962-63 could leave their mark for a year or two. Juniper Bottom held the frost and the lower branches of the yews were brown throughout the summer, and seemed likely to go the way of the juniper they replaced; but 1963 and 1947 had glorious summers to repair the damages of winter. Calcicole shrubs and trees recovered as fast as the sward, Box, privet, dogwood, wayfaring tree, whitebeam and finally the yew, specialists in growing on a chalky soil, are all abundant. On Box Hill they are joined by ash, beech, elder, silver birch, wild cherry and wych elm, that can grow on other soils as well. When you visit Box Hill you can depend on the variegated greens of these

† "The Dancing Bees: An Account of the Life and Senses of the Honey Bee."
* See appendix at end of chapter.

trees in spring and summer, and on the various autumn tints, every bit as much as you can depend on finding stinking hellebore in March, milkwort in May, stemless thistle in July or felwort in September.

A typical season on Box Hill begins in March with the bright green of stinking hellebore, contrasting with the dead brown of last year's beech leaves, and outdoing the shy green flowers of dog's mercury. In April come the wood anemones, soon to be accompanied by the wild ramsons, not on the chalk, but in the woods on the clay, by the Mole or up in Ashurst Rough. Then in May appear other flowers not of the chalk: in a meadow near Wentworth Hall, a mist of the smoky blue and mauve of cuckoo flower or lady's smock; in Ashurst Rough, on the clay, a sea of bluebells with the occasional yellow of archangel and rarer purple of early purple orchid. In our diary for 9.5.54 we have a note: "Two wood warblers were singing in a glade in Ashurst Rough, a cool and beautiful place of beech trees and bluebells, the latter a sudden and wonderful sight. We came across a whole sheet of them beneath a single large beech. The fragrant scent hanging in the woodland air was as lovely as the flowers" — not chalk sward, perhaps, but within a stone's throw of Juniper Top. The Clay-with-Flints of Ashurst Rough permits a host of species to flower where the calcium carbonate of the open down would discourage them. For example in the rides between the oaks and birches, where clay puddles lie, grows the shy star of yellow pimpernel — a stranger to the chalk sward.

As May moves into June the scarp comes more into the picture, and fewer of the flowering species are found among the trees. Bugle comes plunging out of the edges of the woods, while among the sward appear the milkwort and birdsfoot trefoil and ox-eye daisy, and in the verges the rock-rose, or stitchwort, or green spurge or one of the bedstraws; most fragrant of all, the cushions of thyme. Shakespeare spoke of a bank whereon the wild thyme blows, and we have been reciting and singing his words for three and a half centuries. It was no secluded bank along an Arden lane; it was a stretch of chalk or limestone turf such as the Sussex-loving Rudyard Kipling haunted, when he wrote of "our close-bit thyme that smells like dawn in Paradise".

July is the height of the flower season. There is a clearing west of Ranmore where the viper's bugloss grows so tall that from a distance it looks like a border of lupins and delphiniums. Drifts of ox-eye daisy line the floor of the Ashurst Valley. On Juniper Top, our beloved sward, there is birdsfoot trefoil and pink centaury and yellow-wort, and on White Down horseshoe vetch and kidney vetch. Rock-rose, clustered bellflower, agrimony on the edge of the scrub, stonecrop and marjoram begin to join the carpet of thyme, milkwort, flax, squinancywort, salad burnet and the hawkbits. In July come the thistles, stemless and carline, with the less common musk thistle drooping a crimson head, or the spear thistle stabbing upwards. In July also come the parasites, eyebright and rest-harrow and the climbers and twiners — honeysuckle in Ashurst Rough, black bryony and white among the thorn scrub. July is the month for record breaking if you have a weakness for seeing a hundred species in flower in one evening. We made use of our knowledge of the geology of the area to do this in a walk crossing from the Lower Greensand of Wotton, through the Gault of the Holmsdale, up the chalk scarp of Ranmore to the acid sands and gravels of Ranmore Common.

Hedgerow and wayside verge required attention too. Here we found the deep blue-purple of tufted vetch, the woundworts and black horehound, knapweeds and yarrow and ragwort and ever-lasting pea where earlier there had been the delicate skein of cow parsley and the gold of buttercup and dandelion. Mercifully the Surrey County Council abstains from spraying the roadside with weed-killer with the scandalous profusion once seen in some counties. How good that road verges are now being listed as nature reserves to ward off the showers of rate-provided chemicals!

August is the dry month — at least sometimes — the month of holiday-makers and compulsive flower pickers, the month when we never visited Box Hill, the month when the crimsons of the thistles and knapweeds, and the far-away blue of the harebell are in greatest profusion, the month when felwort (with pink centaury and yellow-wort, two other Box Hill gentians) comes into flower. In September and October in the shortening days it was possible to have a revision of many of the flowers of summer. Among the eyebrights and hawk-weeds and autumn ladies' tresses would be a surprising number of second flowerings — mulleins, viper's bugloss, both the centauries and clustered bellflower. Over on the Ranmore side there would be second-bloom foxgloves, and the tremendous snowstorm of seeding rose bay — most spectacular of flowers. Down by the Mole police-man's helmet (Himalayan balsam), still held the banks of the river like film actors enacting Borodino in War and Peace, and everywhere were thistle seeds and the bright berries of whitebeam and wayfaring tree and bramble and dogwood.

Some common flowers have become less common, primroses for certain, and on Box Hill cowslips also. Visitors can hardly be blamed for wanting to pick these lovely flowers, but must never be encouraged to do so. When the population was small then naturally country folk took their nosegays, but the population explosion has changed all this. Once, as we travelled in the train past Ashtead Forest, an old man said to us: "Them woods used to be full of primroses in the spring when I was a lad. Used to get 'em by the basketful. There aren't any now. Can't think why!" We could have told him. We say something about this in the orchid chapter. The picked flower cannot seed. There can be no regeneration.

Certain flowers were especial favourites because they could be relied upon to occur in the same place every year. Outside West Humble Station grows the greater celandine with whose yellow pith you could stain your skin, and the wood spurge along the wood edge, where you could do the same in white. There is the Duke of Argyll's tea plant in West Humble Lane and the little woodruff, and columbine in the Pinehurst woodland, and violets everywhere: enchanter's nightshade in the company of wood sanicle and yellow archangels in the copses. Rarer flowers too, which needed a special expedition to verify each year their continued wellbeing — the tiny little ground-pine, a clump of martagon lilies (were these escapes from some now abandoned garden, or were they truly survivors of the wild flower? It was impossible to say). Then, in mid-July we made a solemn pilgrimage to a bank on which grew not simply field scabious and lesser scabious, but the bluer round-headed rampion — common on the South Downs but rare in Surrey. The list of the commoner flowers would be endless, the list of the rarer ones pointless. Rare flowers already have to be guarded against plant collectors.

Perhaps the vegetation of the steep cliffs overhanging the Mole above Burford Bridge is a real relic of an earlier age. Perhaps, as Geoffrey Hutchings used to say, you might expect to meet Mousterian Man wandering in this primeval forest. Here the chalk is so steep that only yew and box and honeysuckle can grow, and deadly nightshade can colonise temporary pockets formed by the roots of fallen trees. There is a pleasant path skirting the river cliff from the Weypole across to Burford Bridge on the hill side of the stream, from which you can get glimpses down to the river. To climb the slope above needs the agility of the London boy, and the overalls and jeans of the determined scrambler. Here, if anywhere, might flower the relics of a bygone age. The riverside itself is gay with seeded flowers brought down from the Weald on the flood — balsam and meadow cranesbill and hogweed and charlock.

Ultimately however, the greatest delight of Box Hill is the chalk sward and its carpets and cushions of low-lying flowers. This is a very delicately balanced delight. Relax for a moment, and you find it invaded by thorns, by juniper, by yew and by beech, and you are back in what operatic singers would describe as "dark impenetrable forest". It would indeed be a pity if all the North Downs were put under the plough. It would be horrible if they were all planted with alien conifers, but it would be ridiculous if, through over-crowding by human beings they progressed towards desert or, on the other hand, through neglect, reverted completely to forest. It is the task of those in whose care Box Hill lies, to ensure that the chalk sward is preserved, but they will succeed in this only if they receive the intelligent support of people who visit the Hill.

APPENDIX

List of flowers of the chalk scrub most frequently noted in 22 years.
(Figures give number of years in which flower noted.)

22. milkwort and ox-eye daisy
21. rock-rose and clustered bellflower, self-heal, thyme, birdsfoot trefoil
20. St. John's wort (2 spp), yellow-wort, pink centaury, eyebright, knapweed
19. cowslip, strawberry, mouse-ear hawkweed, violet, marjoram, white bedstraw
18. purging flax, agrimony, mignonette, yellow bedstraw
17. lesser scabious, harebell, viper's bugloss, and very frequently — greater scabious, wood-sage, crosswort, rest-harrow, yellow rattle, squinancywort, horseshoe vetch, greater knapweed, round-headed rampion, yellow toadflax, ivy-leafed toadflax, yellow stonecrop, dropwort, kidney vetch, autumn gentian (felwort) and candytuft.

List of flowers of the scrub, woodland and wayside most frequently noted in 22 years.
22. bluebell, field parsley, white dead-nettle, lesser celandine, dandelion.

21. yellow archangels, pink campion, white campion, bladder campion, bugle and wood sanicle.
20. greater celandine, rose-bay willow-herb, enchanter's nightshade, stitchwort
19. ramsons, yellow pimpernel, dog rose
18. cuckoo flower, bittersweet
17. dog's mercury, lesser willow-herb, hedge woundwort, and very frequently: — hogweed, potentilla tormentil, nettle-leaved bellflower, honeysuckle, wood-sage, primrose, tufted vetch, greater willow-herb, deadly nightshade, wood anemone, gromwell, coltsfoot, marsh marigold, stinking hellebore.

These lists are samples only, and frequency of mention in the diary is no measure of quantity on the ground, which varied enormously from year to year. Certain even commoner flowers; bindweeds, bryonies, brambles, buttercups, daisies, groundsels, umbellifers and hawkweeds, plantains and clovers are not mentioned.

CHAPTER SIX
THE ORCHIDS OF BOX HILL

We set out once, a secret party in a land rover, up the lanes of Surrey. The warden of Juniper Hall was our guide. We parked in a lane at the back of the escarpment somewhere near Ranmore, and plunged into a thick copse, first of hazel then of beech, to emerge on hands and knees on the scarp slope, to kneel round the four-inch flower spike of a fly orchid. This almost invisible flower, resembling, it has been suggested, some insect which has been extinct since the Bronze Age, is camouflaged to human eye, with its shining slaty-blue band across the centre of its brownish-purple lip, to give the impression of light reflected from the folded wings of an insect. It was only the second time we had seen a fly orchid, and we were well and truly hooked on orchids! Peter, who had come with us under protest, with memories of the lavish orchid bouquets from films of gangster funerals, and visions of the gorgeous colouring of "No Orchids for Miss Blandish", had expected something several feet high! "Is that all?" he said, when he had at last focused on the plant in question. "Is that what you brought me all this way for?" He certainly was far from hooked, and promises of lady orchids two feet high in east Kent on another occasion did nothing to mollify him. He had driven us twenty-two miles from South London, and was to drive us back as passengers. He thought us mad. Perhaps we were.

There is no doubt that one's first sight of a new wild orchid — of the delicate bee orchid on the chalk sward, or the tiny burnt tip orchid on South Down cliffs, or of the astonishing contortions of the flower spike of monkey, or lizard, or frog, or early spider, or the ballet beauty of the lady orchid in a copse in east Kent, or the delicate waxy white and fragrance of the greater butterfly orchid in a woodland clearing — a first sight of all these gives a thrill to the viewer out of all proportion to the floral magnificence of these enchanting wild flowers. Box Hill is to be praised because no fewer than seventeen out of the possible fifty English species can be seen there some years by the carefully observant visitor. Just when the leaves are fully out on the beeches, and the hedges are hiding willow warblers and whitethroats from sight, when the Cuckoo and the Garden Warbler are ceasing their songs, and the ornithologist finds only the occasional skulking bird, there is this new interest to enthral him. The orchid season is approaching its zenith. None of the chalk flowers get away before you can see them in the uncomfortable way birds do. A suspected Willow Tit will not stay to permit one to make sure whether it is after all only a Marsh Tit; but an orchid cannot get away, and can be examined at leisure to see whether it is fragrant, or green-veined or pyramidal or marsh — unless of course someone picks it first! The ornithologist indeed is compensated for the decline in the volume of bird song as summer advances, by the appearance of a succession of different species of orchid, and can happily become a botanist.

You can tell the week in the year you have reached by examining the chalk sward or the beech woods or the scrubland to see which orchids are over, and which are out, and which are still to come. On Box Hill, you can, with care, identify the following succession. The first to flower (Group One) are the early purple orchid (orchis mascula), twayblade (listera ovata) and bird's nest orchid (neottia nidus-avis). April 30 is the earliest date we have found these species in flower. The latest dates for Box Hill are respectively June 12, July 14 and July 4, so there is some overlap with other groups.

Group Two, following closely behind, consists of white helleborine (cephalanthera damasonium), man orchid (aceras anthropophorum) and green-veined orchid (orchis morio). May 2, May 13 and May 12 are the earliest, and June 28, July 7 and July 4 are the latest days we have recorded these on Box Hill.

Group Three, overlapping One and Two, contains fly orchid (ophrys muscifera or insectifera), fragrant orchid (gymnadenia conopsea), the common spotted orchid (orchis fuchsii) and the greater butterfly orchid (platanthera chlorantha). We have found the fly orchid in flower between May 26 and June 20, fragrant between May 26 and July 14, and butterfly from June 11 to June 28: the spotted orchid at any time from May 25 to July 14.

Group Four (each group follows about a week behind the one in front) will normally have musk orchid (herminium monorchis), bee orchid (ophrys apifera), pyramidal orchid (anacamptis pyramidalis) and frog orchid (coeloglossum viride). We have found musk orchid out on Box Hill between June 7 and early July, bee from June 8 to July 16 according to the earliness of the season, pyramidal from June 12 to July 21, and frog orchid in early July.

There was a difficulty over Group Five, as the two species, lovers of deep shade, normally bloomed during the August holidays. These two, violet helleborine (epipactys purpurata) and broad-leaved helle-

74

borine (epipactys helleborine or latifolia), had a habit of growing with drooping stems all through July, and then suddenly holding their flower spikes upright and flowering. There was one July when we saw in the dusk, late in the month, a broad-leaved helleborine actually in flower near Juniper Hall, and the flashlight photographs then taken filled a gap in our collection. One used to find them readily enough in August on the Chiltern slopes, but to count a Chiltern broad-leaved helleborine in our Box Hill records would be cheating!

There is only one Box Hill species representing the last group. The ladies' tresses are able to withstand the parched conditions of August and September and autumn ladies' tresses (spiranthes spiralis) we found, usually in association with eyebright, between September 15 and September 29. They do come into flower in August, but we were far away from them by then.

Orchids are exciting plants because they are unpredictable. Some years they grow and bloom in profusion, and in other years they have to be searched for assiduously. Nearly everything about them is astonishing and different from other flowers. Many species are rare and miss several years before appearing again in the same location but not on the same spot. They make it worthwhile to visit the same area over and over again for a succession of seasons and a succession of years, as we did on Box Hill every year from 1949 to 1971. Many orchid flowers are delicately coloured. The resemblance of bee and fly orchid to bee and fly is curious and remarkable, though the resemblance of man and butterfly orchid to man and butterfly is far-fetched! Nor did we ever see a frog orchid which resembled its namesake. Orchids are variously scented, and for any town-dweller who has not entirely lost his sense of smell among the stink of petrol and diesel and chlorinated water, it is an interesting operation to see what the fragrance of the fragrant orchid reminds him of, or to decide whether the musk orchid smells of honey or musk. The butter-fly orchid has a much stronger scent by night than by day, for the benefit of night-flying moths, but what does it smell of? The fragrant orchid is equally strong-scented by night or by day and normally the smell is of nectar, but off-peak one is reminded of cats!

Orchid seeds are so small that there is no room for the storage of food reserves, and nothing resembling a normal seedling will appear for years. Leaves appear as a rule not till the third year, and flowers even later. Given average conditions, you might expect spotted and green-veined orchids to flower in the fifth year after germination, bee and butterfly orchids in the eighth to tenth year, bird's nest and white helleborine in the ninth to eleventh, while you could wait between thirteen and fifteen years for a twayblade or autumn ladies' tresses to flower. Wild orchids are thus no use to gardeners. It is stupid to pick them, and it is ignorant to uproot them. They won't grow in garden plot or window-box.

Growth after seed-germination is slow. Normal green plants manufacture their own energy-producing food (such as sugar) by way of the green colouring matter in their leaves known as chlorophyll, but orchids often have no leaves for years. They grow in a partnership or association with fungi called mycorrhiza. Fungi obtain their energy elsewhere, either directly from green plants, when they are parasites upon these plants, or from the dead remains of plants, when they are called saprophytes. Mycorrhizal fungi are saprophytes. The fungi and the orchids begin as enemies with the fungi winning in winter and the orchids in summer, but their relationship slowly develops into one of living together for mutual aid. This relationship is termed "symbiotic". Orchid seed will not develop if the fungi are absent. They are not ordinary flowers. The bringing under cultivation of old chalk sward, teeming with orchids and mycorrhiza — sward which had not been ploughed for many years or which had perhaps never been ploughed — always saddened us, because it meant the disappearance, maybe for ever, of the natural chalk flora with the profusion of orchids that is to be found in such locations. You have only to look at stretches of the South Downs, where only the steepest escarpment escapes the plough, to realise this.

Orchids once established are perennials. Most die down in winter. Flowering can continue for many years. Twayblades have lasted forty years, though bee and fragrant orchids normally flower only once. We watched a group of greater butterfly orchids over a period of twelve years from 1952 in a remote spot near Juniper Bottom. In only three years did the group produce flower spikes, though leaves emerged above the soil more often than that. Some orchid species can rely on vegetative reproduction, but most rely on seed-setting alone. Thus it is wrong to pick them. The more they are picked the fewer there will be in the future. They should never be picked.

One particular orchid, for which the Box Hill area is known, is the bird's nest orchid (neottia nidus-avis). This orchid never produces leaves; it is entirely saprophytic, and likes the steep slopes of a beech-hanger, where its fleshy yellow spikes are almost the only form of life rising through the carpet of leaves. It stores its sustenance in a mass of tubers and roots underground, from which the name bird's nest is given to it. Many people fail to recognise it as a flower at all, and think of it as a parasite like broom-rape, or as a fungus; but it has on closer inspection a yellowish-brown flower with bright yellow pollinia.

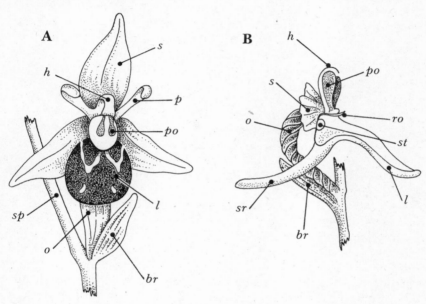

A. Flower of Bee Orchid. B. Half-section of flower of Pyramidal Orchid. B: after Darwin.
British orchids vary so much in shape and detail that it is difficult to select one as representative of all the rest. Nevertheless certain basic features may be discerned. The sepals and petals go in threes and the male and female parts are highly modified. The sepals are easily recognised for they form an outer ring of three and are coloured like petals. Of the petals the lowest one is usually large and is called the lip; it varies considerably in shape among the species. The two upper petals combine and form a hood over the male part of the flower. This consists of two sacs [pollinia] containing pollen grains; the pollinia rest on a platform formed by the rostellum. All that can be seen of the female part is a sticky pad or area [stigma] inside the tubular section of the flower; and the ovary which contains numerous ovules or young seeds. In two British species the tubular section is extended as a spur that contains nectar.

Abbreviations: *br*, bract; *h*, hood; *l*, lip; *o*, ovary; *p*, petal; *po*, pollinium; *ro*, rostellum; *s*, sepal; *sp*, part of spike; *sr*, spur; *st*, stigma.

Colour of the flower spikes is often a misleading feature to anyone beginning to identify orchids. The flower colour does not always denote the species. It is true that certain more stable species like the butterfly orchids or the white helleborine have stabilised their flower colour to cream, or to white with an orange lip, respectively, but many of the other species display all colours from dead white via pale pink to rose and salmon, lilac and deep purple. A group of fragrant or pyramidal orchids may have some pure white specimens among them, while others are pink or purple. Sometimes this is albinism, sometimes it is due to soil deficiency. Albinism is rarer in other species. Sometimes it may be an inherited recessive characteristic. This applies to other flowers besides orchids on Box Hill. There are white bluebells, harebells, bugle, scabious, thistle and milkwort to be found. For orchids albinism can pose some awkward problems. Twice we found a white bee orchid. We have heard tell of albino fly orchids. If the action of cross-fertilisation, of which more anon, is to be successful, then the flower must deceive the male bee or fly into thinking it a female of the same species, and so mount and carry off the pollinia in what has been dubbed "pseudo-copulation". The albino bee or fly orchid will need to find a male bee or fly which likes an albino mate!

Some of the most successful species of orchid have green or yellowish-green or brownish-green flowers — twayblade, broad-leaved helleborine, man orchid, frog orchid, musk orchid to name only five which appear on Box Hill. If they were all flowers of the deep shade, which they are not, one would suspect they would be copying the hellebores and dog's mercury, which flower before the green canopy of the beech trees has come out in the spring; but the last three are flowers of the open sward, and they bloom along with the grasses; the first two like shade, but the broad-leaved helleborine does not flower till August, when the beech canopy is at its thickest. One is tempted to regard these colours as camouflage against the human eye! Certainly the musk orchid is mistaken for flowering grasses and evades being plucked in bunches by orchid plunderers. This camouflage is incidental. Insect eyes are vastly different from human. The object of the shape, smell and colour of a flower seems to be towards procreation and cross-fertilisation for the continuity of the species. For the pollinia of one flower spike to be carried to another of the same species, or even, with certain orchids, to a different species, some wasp, fly, bee or moth must be induced to visit the flower. Usually the search is for nectar or sugar. Occasionally, as described above, it may be shape that attracts the visitor. The mechanism of cross-fertilisation in orchids is a fascinating study, with all the devices in miniature of explosion or booby-trap, or parachute, or sling, or just of stickiness. To study each mechanism really requires a microscope in a laboratory, but the conscientious conservationist must be careful before taking away even single specimens. They may be the only ones! Some orchids develop vegetatively under the soil like daffodils when they are undisturbed, but for those species which rely on seed setting, then cross-fertilisation is better than self-fertilisation.

The bee orchid at one time may have relied on its shape to attract real bees, and so induce the sticky mass of pollen known as the pollinia to be carried on the bee to another flower spike, but, failing that happy result, it has developed a "fail-safe" mechanism by which self-fertilising takes place. The stalks of the pollinia are long and slender. Soon after the flowers open these stalks shrink, and the pollinia are drawn forward out of the stamen, and dangle in front of the stigma. A slight breath of wind then does the job, which the bee or burrowing wasp has failed to do.

A sceptic might doubt whether any real male bee would be so dazzled by longing for the female of his species as to mistake even the most perfect bee orchid for another bee. Bee orchids have relied more and more on self-fertilisation, and so have perpetuated the bad strains and unusual features that militate against the future welfare of the species. This may account for the frequency of albinos and other freaks. An orchid species which relies more on cross-fertilisation, such as the spotted and the marsh orchid, tends to hybridise. Nowhere, so much as among orchids, is the riddle "when is a species a species and when is it a hybrid?" more difficult to answer. The fly orchid, a much rarer and more elusive plant than the bee orchid — indeed we searched for two summers before we found our first specimens — apparently has no mechanism for self-fertilising, when cross-fertilising fails. This would in itself account for the rarity of the plant, and perhaps also for the occurrence of fewer freaks and albinos. If, as has been suggested, the fly orchid really depends for cross-fertilisation merely upon its flower resemblance to a female fly that died out in the Bronze Age, then the fly orchid should have died out in the Bronze Age too! Obviously one ought to sit, day and night in front of a flowering fly orchid, noting the access to it of all insects, and their success or failure in the removal of the pollinia. Unfortunately few amateur botanists would have the health or the patience or the necessary knowledge of entomology to do this. Too few entomologists are botanists as well, and both might need prizing out of their laboratory!

Fly orchid

Professor Summerhayes in his absorbing book "The Wild Orchids of Britain", Number 19 in the Collins' New Naturalist Series, gives many examples of the mechanism of cross-fertilisation. The common twayblade can be cited as an example. Small flies and beetles are attracted by the nectar. They crawl up a groove in the lip of the twayblade flower, and when they touch the part known as the "rostellum", a kind of internal explosion is set off. A small drop of sticky liquid is forced out and gums up the insect's head and the pollinia. Within two or three seconds the sticky mass sets hard, and the frightened insect flies off, probably to a different flower spike, to which it transfers the pollinia, and the trap is set again! Each orchid species has variations, which are dealt with in this fascinating book. One could spend many happy hours with magnifying glass or camera crawling about the chalk sward or the beech hangers of Box Hill inspecting these devices.

Box Hill must be one of the very best orchid locations, or group of locations, in the whole of England. The hill owes this to its calcareous slopes on the Upper and Lower Chalk, where some species favour the sward and some beechwoods or scrubland or oak copse and bluebell wood. Every single year since 1952 we have found twayblade, white helleborine, bird's nest orchid, musk, fragrant and spotted orchids, pyramidal and bee orchids, though of course in far greater numbers some years than others. Man orchid has always been present, and we would always have found early purple orchid, broad-leaved helleborine and autumn ladies' tresses if we had gone to the right places at the right times. More elusive have been fly orchids, which we have found in eight years, violet helleborine in five, greater butterfly orchid in three. Green-veined and frog orchid bring up the rear with one year each, and there have been reports of rarer orchids — burnt-tip among them — which cannot really be described any longer as among the flowers of Box Hill.

The departure of the rabbit after the myxomatosis epidemic of 1953 changed many things. The grass grew longer, and the young hawthorns grew up, and the dogwood scrub spread. This tended to limit the areas of short sward, preferred by musk, frog, green-veined, bee and autumn ladies' tresses: it gave more scope to those orchids which like longer grass — fragrant, pyramidal, and spotted orchids. The practice of coppicing has often in Kent led to eruptions of butterfly and even lady orchids in areas where they have lain dormant for many years, and then sprung into flower at the sudden access of light. Something of the same sort occurred on the northern slopes of Juniper Top, when the spread of dogwood scrub proved such a menace to those entrancing short-turfed slopes. Fortunately, as already related, volunteer parties from Youth Movements set about the dogwood scrub and the clearings thus made have been glorious with fragrant and spotted, twayblade and man orchid since then. Perhaps the loss of the rabbit was not such a bad thing for the orchids. Rabbits used to wander along sampling everything regardless. Failing to find Brer Rabbit's favourite, asparagus, they turned to fragrant orchids. Their absence has for the moment tilted the balance away from musk and burnt-tip towards pyramidal and fragrant orchid.

The forestry management of Box Hill has always provided for areas of woodland and scrub edge on the skirts of steep slopes. At the bottoms of the slopes one would look for man orchid; on the edge of the shade one would seek the fly orchid. Half way up well-drained turf slopes would be musk orchids, and near the tops, six weeks later and usually in association with eyebright, would come autumn ladies' tresses. Musk orchids and autumn ladies' tresses are tolerant of drought and have deep roots. Beech woods provide the habitat for white helleborine, and if the trees are growing on a steep enough slope, for bird's nest orchids. Oak woods would have early purple orchids among their bluebells, and later violet helleborine. Broad-leaved helleborine grows in both localities, while clearings sometimes enable the greater butterfly orchid, one of the loveliest, to flower; but butterfly orchids are found in greater profusion beyond Ranmore towards Horsley and out of our area. We have found clearings in hazel copses where the lady orchid would be at home, but Box Hill is too far west, and you have to go to east Kent for the lady. Military orchids (Chilterns and Cambridge) and red helleborine (Gloucestershire) are even rarer orchids in England, that constant patrolling of Box Hill might one day discover.

These flowers are beautiful to see. Darwin even found one of them, the white helleborine, good to taste. During his study of the orchids of Kent, he related that the orange edge of the white lip tasted of vanilla! An outburst of orchid-chewing has not resulted from this discovery. If it were to occur, then no doubt we could get the dental authorities to rule it out as deleterious to the children's teeth or botanists' dentures!

The glint of purple among a blue sea of bluebells, the candelabra of delicate storeyed bee and fly, the spike of tiny yellow hooded men, the long greenish-white spur of the butterfly, the twisted cream spirals of the ladies' tresses are a joy to see — not once in a lifetime, but over and over again as the seasons and years pass. For all these one must praise Box Hill. As early as 1548 William Turner in his "Names of Herbs" had already identified twayblade and autumn ladies' tresses. There could have been four hundred and thirty years of enjoyment for the observant!

For her orchids, then, let us praise Box Hill. Long may they grow there for our descendants to enjoy.

CHAPTER SEVEN
THE ANIMALS AND INSECTS OF BOX HILL

Box Hill has a great deal more to offer to the naturalist than the birds and flowers on which, as they held a special appeal for us, as they do for many people, we have written at some length. Of particular interest is the rich and varied insect life of which no visitor to the place can fail to be aware. There are many beautiful butterflies, numerous moths for those who know where to look for them, the interesting collections of bright little beetles on the flowery platforms of the wild carrots and other umbelliferous plants, many kinds of spiders and pretty little snails whose many-coloured shells may be collected by the handful in the dry grass under the thorn bushes. The Box Hill area has indeed, long been known as a classic area for the entomologist.

This is well illustrated by a little book published over a century ago, in 1856. It is a kind of entomologist's guide to the London area, written in the form of a calendar, with a chapter for every month. The author, Richard Shield, chose Box Hill as one of his collecting grounds for June. "Let us betake ourselves," he writes, "to the London Bridge Station of the South-Eastern Railway, and, providing ourselves with tickets for the Box Hill Station* on the Reigate, Guildford and Reading Branch, we shall, after about an hour and a quarter's riding through some of the most beautiful scenery in the vicinity of London, arrive at our destination, one of the most prolific localities in rarities both Entomological and Botanical, and embracing the most beautiful scenery with which I am acquainted."

There is something very touching in the thought of this old mid-nineteenth century naturalist travelling to Box Hill from London Bridge Station, just as we did a hundred years later, treading the same ways, delighting in the same lovely places, their wild flowers and trees, their moths and butterflies. Though long dead, his hand seems to reach out, his voice to be heard, across the years and one seems to walk alongside him on the route he follows. It leads to a locality which he calls "the Sanctum Sanctorum" of the entomologist, "the Hilly Field at Headley Lane". To reach this magic place one leaves the Lane by a path just past a farm which must be Warren Farm. "The Hilly Field" must therefore have been somewhere near Wentworth Hall. The path from the lane traverses round the bluff on

* This was the present Deepdene Station at Dorking. (See chapter eleven.)

which the Hall stands and drops steeply down into the dip where the two combes which lie on the western side of Headley Heath, meet. These two combes are rich in insect life of all kinds so perhaps Shield's happy hunting ground was here.

One would like to know more about Richard Shield but his book reveals no personal details. It does tell us much of the man himself however. He was clearly a tremendous enthusiast, a typical Victorian naturalist with his great zest for scientific knowledge and his belief in a Divine plan in which even the lowliest creature had its part to play. Like the vast majority of the naturalists of the time he was an avid collector, out to "bag" as many specimens as he could. His book reflects the age also in its use of scientific nomenclature. To identify the insects, mainly moths, of which he writes, one has to thumb painstakingly through the index of Latin names in the books. He must have been a lively companion and a bit of a wag. Writing of one of his captures he describes it as "the gem of the Headley Lane, the best plum in the micro-lepidopterological pudding". (This was the larva of Coleophora conspicuella, a tiny little moth, one of a numerous family of which he found several other species on Box Hill.)

Shield took particular pleasure in these little moths whose Latin names — they rarely have English ones — are as long as the moths themselves are small. To him Box Hill was an entomologist's paradise where he found many specimens of them. (It would be an interesting exercise for an entomologist today to follow his route and see how many of the species Shield lists could still be found there.) He mentions a few of the large moths — the Lobster, the Crimson Underwing and the Dotted Chestnut for example — but his real enthusiasm is reserved for these tiny creatures, many of them no bigger than clothes moths, requiring a pocket lens to see them properly. Many are dull little insects but others, when closely examined, are extremely beautiful, Chrysoclista linneella for instance, which has brightly coloured wings and is no larger than a blue-bottle, and the Yponomeutidae. There are also the exquisite little white plume moths which one is almost sure to see flitting about in the grass on summer evenings. Shield lists no less than seven different species of this family which he found on Box Hill.

The larvae of these moths feed on plants which are common on Box Hill, the two knapweeds, St. John's wort, the various hawkweeds, stitchwort, spindle, bramble, birch, whitebeam for example, and, of course, the grasses. Some of them are leaf miners or stem borers. Others roll the leaves of plants into cylinders in which they live and feed. Sometimes the little caterpillars are so numerous as to reach pest proportions, for example those of the Tortricidae which dangle on long threads from the oaks on which they feed in Ashurst Rough. They sometimes quite defoliate these trees at the same time providing abundant food for the birds, titmice, sparrows and flocks of garrulous starlings.

It would be the study of a lifetime to get to know and learn to identify all the moths to be found even in so small an area as Box Hill. There are dedicated entomologists who do succeed, through their enthusiasm and their devotion, in achieving such rare distinction. Such a one was Richard Shield. We ourselves were exceptionally fortunate in having amongst our friends no less than four such gifted and accomplished men who sometimes joined us on our evening walks on Box Hill. They never failed to astonish us with their facility in identifying these little moths and by revealing the number of different species there are to be found by those who know how and where to look for them. They taught us the names of a few of them, waves and carpets, thorns and plumes, pugs and geometers and others with Latin names which we promptly forgot.

The larger moths, such as the hawk moths, are much easier to recognise but we saw comparatively few of these, Humming Bird Hawk and Cream Spot Tiger, the latter in the Norbury woods, being our best records. Undoubtedly the moth which is most often seen on Box Hill is the Six — sometimes Seven — Spot Burnet. It is a beautiful little creature with wings of polished dark green, set with vivid red spots and red underwings which show when it flies. Its habit of frequenting the lovely azure flowers of viper's bugloss enhances its attractiveness. The sight of numbers of these pretty little moths flitting about the tall spikes of the bugloss on some sunny afternoon, is one of the most charming Box Hill affords. Another daylight-flying moth, the Cinnabar, which is crimson and black, may also be seen on Box Hill, as may its conspicuous black and orange caterpillars, feeding on ragwort.

Box Hill has its own characteristic butterfly population. Not surprisingly grassland-haunting species tend to predominate. Chief amongst these are the Common Blue and the Meadow Brown, the two butterflies one sees most frequently. The Meadow Brown may be seen fluttering in erratic flight over open grassy places in any month between May and September. It is one of the few butterflies which does not seem to object to inclement weather. Crossing the hill in rain or mist one will see them flying over the saturated grasses when no other butterflies are abroad. On sunny days however it is the common blues which catch the eye. When they are about in numbers they add beauty and life to the scene. Coming down the steep side of the Zig-Zag one evening in late May we found that there had been a recent hatch of common blues. We could see them all about us, hanging like small blue flowers to the tips of the grass stems. Below were the fragile empty cases of the chrysalids from which the butterflies had just emerged. Despite its name and such occurrences as that described we do not consider this butterfly common in the sense that it may regularly be seen in large numbers.

Other butterflies, all characteristic of grass or heath land, which are likely to be seen on Box Hill in most years, are the Small Copper, Small Heath, Ringlet and four members of the skipper family, the Large, the Small, the Grizzled and the Dingy Skippers. The Dingy Skipper, whose larvae feed on birdsfoot trefoil, is possibly less often seen than the other three. Of the other grassland haunting butterflies, the Wall, Grayling, Gatekeeper, Brown Argus and Green Hairstreak are all likely to be seen in the area. Butterflies which prefer woodland or the margins of woodland and which are not uncommon on Box Hill are the Speckled Wood and the Small Pearl-bordered Fritillary. The latter appears in some seasons in fair numbers when they may be found basking on the sun-warmed paths down the combes. Almost invariably they flit away as one approaches. More rarely seen is the handsome little Duke of Burgundy Fritillary. We once found the caterpillars of the High Brown Fritillary but were never fortunate enough to see the butterfly itself.

The first butterfly to appear in the spring, the Brimstone, is fairly common on and around Box Hill. This is a matter over which to rejoice, for it is always a delight to see, on some warm sunny day in late March or early April, the first of the brimstones, its delicate sulphur-yellow colour seeming to reflect the pure, pale yellow of the catkins on the sallows and the primroses which grow beneath them. We had records of brimstones in all months from March to July. The Orange Tip, another spring butterfly, we recorded less frequently than the Brimstone and only in the months of April, May and June. The Small Tortoiseshell and the Peacock we found evenly distributed in a variety of habitats but the Red Admiral and the Comma we considered to be comparatively uncommon on Box Hill itself. Possibly the gardeners of Mickleham and West Humble see these two butterflies more frequently for they are both lovers of the flower border. Other species of which we had only one or two records for Box Hill were the White Admiral, Painted Lady, Green-veined White and Clouded Yellow. Possibly the fact that we never visited the Hill in August, which is a good month for butterflies, accounts for the paucity of our records of these and one or two other species. It was a disappointment to us never to record the Marbled White on Box Hill. We found it to be quite common on the Chilterns, where the environment is similar to that of the North Downs.

As with the moths, so with other forms of insect life, we were sure of some of the larger ones but puzzled by most of the smaller creatures. Any observant visitor to Box Hill will speedily become aware of the great wealth of the smaller forms of life which abounds there. In the words of Richard Shield "countless thousands sport their little day, and do the work appointed them to do". There are ants of various kinds, several types of bees and wasps, including wood wasps, scorpion flies, a number of interesting beetles, such as the soldier beetle, the bloody-nosed beetle and the cardinal beetle, and a variety of fascinating spiders including harvest spiders, many grasshoppers of course and numerous engaging little creatures such as the armadillidium, which rolls itself into a ball, like a hedgehog, when disturbed.

Apart from the butterflies there are a few larger insects with which the constant visitor to Box Hill is sure to become acquainted. Big dragon-flies with shimmering wings and bodies of brilliant metallic colouring shoot past, far from the water in which they were born. On warm summer evenings cockchafers, sometimes called June bugs, appear, often in considerable numbers. The clumsy, booming things fairly bombard one at times. It is quite hard work batting them away and one regards with unqualified approval the sight of the big noctule bats, weaving in powerful flight above and hopes they are taking full toll of the irritating 'chafers. Another common insect whose appearance is always greeted without enthusiasm is the horse fly or clegg. Those who suffer poisoned limbs when bitten by these unpleasant creatures, do well to remain on the more wind-swept parts of the Hill when they are about, avoiding the warm, sheltered hollows where the brutes lurk. A much smaller insect, the harvest mite, which is common in the grass in late summer, can also inflict

88

extremely irritating bites on those incautious enough to sit on the ground. They are a great nuisance altogether, as it is in this warm and pleasant part of the year that one most enjoys reclining on some sunny, thyme-scented slope. Even if one keeps on the move however one can still pick them up, just walking through the grass, so it pays to wear boots, much though it goes against inclination in dry summer weather.

Two of the most interesting of the larger insects to be found on Box Hill, the glow-worm and the stag beetle, have unfortunately, become rare in recent years. We never regarded glow-worms as at all common and found them less so as time went on. However a friend who stayed at Burford Bridge in July 1965 told us that the slope behind the Hotel was alight with them on two successive nights while another friend recalls seeing the path up the scarp above Betchworth brightly illuminated by them one evening in 1948, so possibly we would have recorded them more frequently had we been able to remain longer after dusk. It may be significant that the place where we most often saw glow-worms was the sides of the cutting in which Box Hill Station lies. We always used to look for them there while waiting for the train back to London. Perhaps by then others would have lit their little lamps along the ways we had been following earlier in the evening.

In our first few years on Box Hill we several times saw specimens of that large and magnificent creature, the stag beetle, the Pincher

Stag beetle

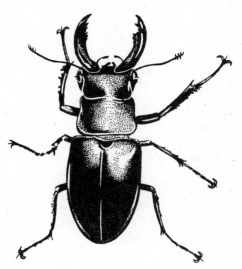

Bob of the country folk. It is Britain's largest beetle. Great, clumsy-looking things, purplish-black in colour, they fly very slowly, trundling along like antiquated aircraft and are easily recognised. The males are heavily horned which gives them a ferocious appearance but they are quite harmless. Nevertheless the sight of one of them as it comes lumbering along at about head height can be somewhat daunting to those who have never encountered one before. It was a disappointment to us that after the summer of 1953 we saw them no more on Box Hill.

The big Roman snails, which we found quite common in the earlier years of our walks on Box Hill, also became less numerous as time went on. A possible explanation which has been suggested for this is that they were being eaten by foxes, turning to other forms of food following the reduction in rabbit numbers after the myxomatosis epidemic. Box Hill, like all chalk and limestone areas, has a wealth of smaller snails, many of them very prettily marked. They are easily found by rooting about under bushes or in the long grass in hollows and hedge bottoms. Sometimes one will see whole clusters of them on some tall plant such as hedge parsley or wild carrot.

We often discussed the question of whether there had been a decline in the insect population of Box Hill during the twenty or so years in which we were regularly visiting it. On the whole we felt that there had. The disappearance of the stag beetle and the reduction in the numbers of Roman snails and possibly glow-worms as well, has been already remarked. The numbers of many insects can fluctuate markedly from year to year of course. Cockchafers, for example, were numerous in 1952 and 1965 while in 1954 we saw none. It was a wet summer that year and butterfly numbers were also noticeably low. Overall our impression was that there were fewer butterflies in the late 1960's than there had been in the early 1950's but it is not a matter on which it is easy to be positive. Box Hill is not subject to spraying or indeed to any form of application of chemicals. The native flora, on which the larvae of the butterflies or other insects feed, is not interfered with, except by the trampling of human feet or the fires which occur from time to time, usually as a result of some form of carelessness, on Headley Heath. Possibly, as with the changes in bird life, a minor fluctuation in climate may be the cause of a decline in the numbers of some insect species. There is evidence that our climate has become slightly

90

wetter and milder in recent years. Many insects do better when winters are colder, summers hotter and drier, than they were in the last ten years of our acquaintance with Box Hill. Perhaps we were fortunate to have been able to spend so much time there in the decade of the 'fifties, when the evenings had such particular enchantment, the wild life so rich and varied. There is a verse in William Collins' "Ode to Evening" which exactly recaptures the mood of that time.

> *"Now air is hush'd, save where the weak-eyed bat*
> *With short shrill shriek flits by on leathern wing,*
> *Or where the beetle winds*
> *His small but sullen horn."*

Of the larger forms of wild life, the four-footed mammals and reptiles, those most likely to be seen on Box Hill are the fox, the rabbit and the grey squirrel. Down below the Hill, beside the Mole, the water vole is common. The fox is a wary, rather than shy, animal. It is much more likely to be watching you than the other way round. Now and again one will catch a glimpse of a dark red shadow crossing one of the rides in Ashurst Rough or disappearing beneath the yew trees on the other side of one of the combes. However the regular visitor to Box Hill will be fairly sure of seeing one eventually, before it has seen or winded him. It depends a good deal on what the fox is doing. We once watched one for several minutes, trotting down the side of the Ashurst Valley from Juniper Top. It was sniffing about in the long grass like an excited dog, perhaps searching for mice. One of the prettiest sights we ever saw on Box Hill was of two fox cubs playing together around an old log. We had struggled up the side of one of the combes through thick beech and yew woodland and emerged on a little plateau, thick with rose-bay willow herb whose heavy, honey-like scent filled the air. Tall trees grow all round the edges of the little plateau, cutting it off from view from other parts of the Hill. This and its inaccessibility make it an unfrequented, secret sort of place. The fox cubs seemed aware of this for they were behaving in a completely natural manner, quite unafraid. Eventually they spotted us as we crept nearer. One ran off at once into the cover behind the log. The other, a bolder or more inquisitive animal, sat down on its haunches like a puppy, ears pricked, watching us with interest before it too ran off to join its playmate in the tangle back of the log.

In the early autumn evenings the foxes become noisy and we have often come down from the Hill in the gathering dusk to the accompaniment of the sharp yapping of the dog foxes and the weird shrieks of the vixens. One such occasion remains particularly clear in recollection. It was a dull late September evening, with low cloud blanketing the sky and dusk falling quickly. Mist was creeping up the combes, causing the outlines of trees and bushes to become indistinct. There was no wind and the countryside was still and silent apart from the brown owls which had begun to call tunefully in the woods on Lodge Hill and around Pinehurst. Presently two, possibly three, dog foxes began to yap. When the vixens joined in with their screaming cries the noise became unearthly. Together with the hooting of the owls it was quite a concert, the total effect of which was distinctly eerie. Under its influence and that of the rising mist the slope from Juniper Top to the Headley Lane lost its familiar aspect and seemed to become primeval. One imagined the shadows of Stone Age hunters abroad in the yew forest, wolf and wild boar creeping down to the Mole to drink. As Shakespeare wrote,

" . . . in the night, imagining some fear,
How easy is a bush suppos'd a bear!"

Though so near to London Box Hill can be a very lonely place at times. No doubt the foxes prefer it that way.

The only other comparatively large mammal which makes its home on Box Hill is the badger. It is far less often seen than the fox yet one is continually aware of its presence. There are at least a dozen badger 'hills' in the area. These can be recognised by the size of the holes the animals excavate and the mounds of earth and piles of disused bedding they throw out from them. There are always a number of holes in close proximity to one another in these 'hills'. One comes across them when one leaves the regular paths and penetrates the yew forests or the more secluded parts of the deciduous woodlands. The badgers also leave recognisable tracks. Creatures of regular habits, they rarely stray from their accustomed paths, which form narrow, twisting runways threading the undergrowth and scrub. They are particularly noticeable where they come down some steep bank to cross a road or lane.

As already remarked it is rarely that one is fortunate enough to

Badger

see a badger — without, that is sitting up half the night over-looking one of the 'hills'. We saw them on only two occasions, both of these when we were searching for orchids. The first of these was on a June evening when, as we proceeded slowly along the side of one of the combes we heard rustlings from beneath the thick screen of yew trees which lay above us. Creeping cautiously to a point where we could peer into the sunlight-dappled shade beneath the yews we were delighted to see two badgers rooting about industriously on the bare, flint-strewn ground. With their pearly-grey coats and black and white striped heads they made a fine sight in such a setting. We watched them for several minutes before some slight sound one of us made alerted them to our presence and in an instant they were gone. The other occasion was on the far side of the Mole on the Norbury slopes when one of us almost trod on a badger which must have been lying asleep in the long grass. It departed uphill at speed, grunting and growling its disapproval at being so rudely disturbed.

Box Hill is a badger sanctuary. If the Hill were to be preserved for no other reason than this it would be worth doing. It is incredible that in this supposedly enlightened age there are still men so ignorant and brutal as to kill, in the cruellest manner, this interesting and harmless animal. Thank goodness that a law has recently been passed extending some measure of protection to the badger. Thank goodness also for the National Trust and an understanding public which, on Box Hill at least, give it protection and leave it free to follow its ancient ways unmolested.

There seems little doubt that another once much persecuted animal, the otter, is now no longer to be seen in the Box Hill area except on the rarest occasions. One of the water bailiffs told us that he had once seen one by the Mole but could not recollect how long ago. Denham Jordan, the Dorking naturalist, who wrote under the nom-de-plume of Son of the Marshes, gives a vivid account in one of his books, "On Surrey Hills", of watching otters at play in the Mole by night. This was probably below Hox Hill for he writes of the otter in another of his books, "Where the steep sides of the hill — called the Whites — shoot down to the river, he is at home." Victim of persecution in the past and pressure on the countryside today, the otter is now most unlikely to be seen beside the Mole, though the chance of one turning up there cannot be entirely excluded. Like the badger, the otter is faithful to its ancient haunts and an occasional wanderer appears where they were once always to be found.

Another water-loving animal, the water vole, may still be seen anywhere along the Mole between the Weypole and the approaches to Leatherhead. It is a pity that the water vole, which is a harmless and engaging little animal, is so often mis-called the water rat, for it thereby most undeservedly shares some of the unpopularity attaching to that unattractive creature, the brown rat. The youths whom we sometimes met, prowling by the Mole with air rifles, when questioned, almost invariably told us that they were rat-shooting. We could only hope that the difference between the round-headed, plump little vole and the brown rat, with its narrow head, beady eyes, yellow teeth and long, naked tail, was as apparent to them as they always assured us it was.

The water vole is usually seen as a small, beaver-like creature, swimming across the river to the safety of the far bank, having sensed the approach of an intruder to its domain. Often one spots it first by seeing the spreading wake its passage leaves on the placid surface of the water. Caught unawares it is a most interesting little animal. One which we watched for some minutes one evening near the Weypole, was eating the stem of a reed. In the stillness by the gently-flowing river we could plainly hear the sound of its rapid munching. Presently it dropped its piece of reed and swam to a bit of driftwood onto which it climbed and began to wash its face, a picture of innocence no brown rat could have achieved. Through binoculars it was possible to note the rusty tint of the hair on its head and the delicate purple sheen of the fur on its back.

Rabbits used to be plentiful on Box Hill before the myxomatosis outbreak. One never saw them in great numbers but the evidence of their presence was there in the close-cropped sward. After the myxomatosis epidemic we continued to see rabbits here and there so they were by no means wiped out. The thickening grasses and the spreading scrub showed however, how greatly their numbers had been reduced.

Hares were less numerous and more restricted in their distribution than rabbits. We never saw one on Box Hill itself but recorded them regularly in the farmlands above Pebblecombe. We also saw them now and again in the meadows by the Mole and the fields to the west of the river. Similarly with deer, we had no records for Box Hill but the sighting of roedeer on Ranmore Common and once in a meadow by the Mole show that they are present in the area. These shy animals probably find Box Hill too much thronged by human beings for their liking.

Of the smaller animals, weasels are likely to be seen by the quiet watcher on Box Hill but the stoat seems rare. We had only one record of it in twenty years. Mice, shrews and voles of various species, are common though of course not often seen, being small and shy. The hedghog, though not a particularly shy animal, is not likely to be seen with much frequency as it is largely nocturnal in habit. Nor, as it spends most of its time underground, is the mole. Now and again one will appear on the surface of the ground. We once saw one do so on the Mickleham cricket ground, while a match was actually in progress. The little black creature appeared all of a sudden, running in short spurts, like a clockwork mouse. Play temporarily came to a halt until it was removed.

The most conspicuous of the smaller animals found on Box Hill is that impudent exhibitionist and successful cadger, the grey squirrel. It is not possible to be dogmatic on the matter but our

95

impression is that grey squirrels increased in number during the twenty years we were making regular visits to the area. As any visitor to Box Hill knows, they are numerous around the cafés where they find good pickings. They are industrious scavengers, prepared to try anything which appears edible. We once watched one eating a banana skin. In and about the cafés and other places where people congregate they show little fear of human beings. In the less frequented parts of the woodlands however, they behave more like wild creatures, scampering away at one's approach. On such occasions they can be surprisingly clumsy. We have more than once seen one miss its footing in its panic-stricken dash through the branches and come crashing to the ground. However this never seems to do them any harm. Almost as soon as they hit the earth they are up and away. They also show an astonishing capacity for getting run over. It is by no means unusual to come across their corpses by the roadside. Apart from such mischances the grey squirrel leads a carefree life for it lacks natural predators though an occasional one may be taken by an owl. We viewed its numbers on Box Hill with some concern, knowing its propensity for discovering and devouring the eggs and nestlings of the birds in which we took such delight. Its capacity for damaging and even killing trees is referred to in a later chapter. Engaging little animal though it may be the grey squirrel is in fact a pest and should not be encouraged.

Apart from the pipistrelle and the noctule, the smallest and the largest of British bats, we did not have many records of bats for Box Hill. Pipistrelles we often saw, flickering round the cedars on the Juniper Hall lawns or amongst the trees by the Mole. These and the noctules are not difficult to identify. Others baffled us. One, seen flying up and down the tunnel of trees above the Mole in broad daylight, had a dark chestnut back and head, tawny-cream underparts and blue-grey wings. Another we saw was dull brown in colour with grey wings. We were unable to decide to what species these two bats belonged but their presence in the area suggests that it has possibilities for the naturalist who is particularly interested in this branch of the animal kindgom.

We had a special liking for the big noctules. There is a suggestion of something fierce and predatory about them, a touch of the pterodactyl, giving one the feeling of having moved back in time to a day when man's domination of the earth and his resulting capacity for harming it were yet to come. They usually hunt in parties, some-

above and below: Two inviting paths through typical orchid terrain on Box Hill.

Man Orchid.

Bird's Nest Orchids.

Some of the various species of orchids which may be found on Box Hill.

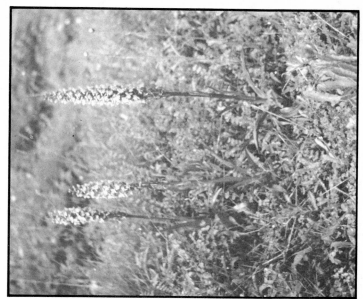

Fragrant Orchids.

Butterfly Orchid.

Musk Orchids.

Fly Orchid.

Pyramidal Orchids.

Spotted Orchid.

Mullein, one of the taller wild flowers of the chalk.

Early Purple Orchid.

Two forms of wild life, the innocent and the not-so-innocent, found on Box Hill.

left: Grey Squirrel.
(*Photo: Mike Frost*)

below: Peacock Butterfly.
(*Photo: Mike Frost*)

above: Juniper Hall, where General D'Arblay courted Fanny Burney.
below: Flint Cottage, below the Zig-Zag, where George Meredith lived for many years and wrote some of his best-known works.

times as many as twenty strong, making one think of the packs of flying foxes or fruit bats, to be seen in the tropics. Their favourite hunting grounds seem to be above the hilltops. We used to see them over Juniper Top and Lodge Hill as well as the scarp of Box Hill itself. It is a fine sight to see a group of these big bats, circling, sweeping, turning and dipping against the pale blue evening sky. The flight is strong and rapid, lacking the erratic character of that of the smaller bats. Sometimes we saw noctules and swifts racing about the sky together. Then, as the light faded, the swifts would disappear, leaving the noctules hunting alone. We would watch them until the light had all but gone and we could see them no longer. We used to wonder if they continued to hunt throughout the night and where, when their hunting was over, they hung themselves up to sleep.

Visitors to Box Hill who do not care for snakes will be pleased to know that, as far as our observations go, the adder is absent from the locality. They are fairly common on Leith Hill which provides the sort of dry, heathy environment they prefer. We occasionally saw grass snakes in the lower-lying, damper places. On Box Hill itself the reptile one is most likely to see is the common lizard. Usually one has no more than a glimpse of it as it scuttles away out of sight but now and again, if one moves slowly and quietly, one may be lucky enough to see one, momentarily still, on some warm stone or patch of bare earth in the dry, sunny places they favour.

In this chapter we have written mainly about those creatures, animals, reptiles or insects, which we ourselves encountered in our many visits to Box Hill. No attempt has been made to give an account of every wild thing which might be found there. This would require a specialised book, such as John Sankey's 'Chalkland Ecology', which contains lists of the various forms of life, both vegetable and animal, to be discovered in the chalk country, with many direct references to Box Hill. What we have tried to do is to show what a rich variety of natural life may still be found there by anyone who is prepared to walk a little slowly, perhaps to sit awhile, watching and listening.

CHAPTER 8
THE LITERARY ASSOCIATIONS OF BOX HILL.
CAMDEN TO DEFOE

Many great names in English literature have associations with Box Hill. The view from the North Downs scarp, the dramatic gorge of the Mole, the crossing place of Roman Stane Street and the prehistoric track now known as the Pilgrims' Way, the beauty of Box Hill itself, all barely twenty miles from London, have attracted the attention of numerous writers in various fields. The peculiar legend of the disappearing Mole particularly intrigued the earliest of these, Camden, Fuller, Aubrey and Celia Fiennes;Fanny Burney and George Meredith lived at the foot of the hill; Keats wrote about the scenery in 'Endymion'; Robert Louis Stevenson sensed the romance of the old inn called The Fox and Hounds, now the Burford Bridge Hotel, and was tempted to write another 'Kidnapped' about it; Jane Austen is thought to have made Leatherhead the scene of 'Emma' and brought Emma and her friends to picnic on Box Hill. Of the travellers and diarists Pepys got no nearer than Epsom but Evelyn came over from Wotton to see the trees; Celia Fiennes twice rode past, followed shortly afterwards by Defoe, both more intrigued by the behaviour of the Mole than the beauty of the scenery. John Wesley had proselytes at Dorking and had eyes more for their salvation than the countryside around while William Cobbett turned his back on Box Hill in order to admire the crops at its foot. Eighteenth century writers in the Gentleman's Magazine delighted in the fine country seats and parklands around Dorking. The early twentieth century produced the literary archaeologists, like Hilaire Belloc, tracing the Pilgrims' Way, or S.E. Winbolt and I.D. Margary, pursuing the route of Stane Street. Finally there are the ecologists, botanists and geologists of our own time, Lousley and Walters, Wooldridge and Hutchings, for example.

The earliest reference in our literature to Box Hill and the river Mole which skirts it comes from the 'Britannia' of William Camden. Camden was an Oxford man who went on to become Headmaster of Westminster School. During the vacations he toured England collecting information for his geographical and historical survey which he began at the age of twenty and spent fifteen years writing. The first edition, written in Latin, was published in 1586. Another scholar, Doctor Philemon Holland, put this Elizabethan best-seller into the formal English of the period. A contemporary gave it this commendation: 'Men have called this book the common sun, whereat our modern writers have all lighted their little torches.' In other words authors have quoted from Camden from that day to this and we shall be no exception. It was the river and the legend of its peculiar behaviour which attracted his attention rather than the hill. The 1610 English edition reads: 'Within some few miles the River Mole, having from the south side passed through the whole country, hasteneth to join the Thamis; but at length being letted by over-thwart hills, maketh himself a way underground in the manner of a mouldwarp, like unto the famous River Anas in Spain: whereof it may seem it took name, seeing that creature living within the ground is called also in English a Mole.

The Mole being now come as far as White Hill, whereon the box tree groweth in great plentie, at the foote thereof hideth himselfe, or rather is swallowed up, and thereof the place is called the Swallow: but after a mile or two neere unto Letherhed Bridge boiling and breaking forth, taketh joy to spring oute againe. So that the inhabitants of this tract may boast as well as the Spaniards, that they have a bridge which feedeth many flockes of sheepe: for this is a common by-word, most rife in the Spaniards' mouths, as toucning the place where their river Anas, now called Guardiana, hideth himselfe for ten miles together. Thus our Mole rising up fresh hasteneth faire and softly by Stoke Dabernon . . . and then very neare Molesey, whereunto it giveth name, sheadeth himself into the Tamis.' Camden then goes on to relate the legend of the duck which was said to have been forced into one of the swallows and came out at the far end with all its feathers removed, proving the existence of the underground course of the river.

With regard to Camden's idea that the name of the River Mole derived from its supposed habit of burrowing underground, G.E. Hutchings has pointed out that in the Middle Ages the name was not Mole but the 'Emlyn Stream' and that the name Mole has been derived in more recent times by 'back formation' from the name Molesey where the river joins the Thames.

Another antiquarian scholar, a contemporary of Camden's, Thomas Fuller, repeated the story of the underground river in his 'Wonders of Surrey' though he plainly had reservations about the story of the duck — or goose, as it is in his version.

'There is a river in this county which at a place called the Swallow sinketh into the earth, and surgeth again some two miles off near Leatherhead; so that it runneth not in an intire stream but as it can find and force its passage the interjacent distance under the earth. I listen not to the country people telling it was experimented by a goose, which was put in and came out again with life (but without feathers): but hearken seriously to those who judiciously impute the subsidency of the earth in the interstice aforesaid to some underground hollowness made by the water in the passage thereof. This river is more properly termed Mole than that in Spain is on like occasion called Anas, that is duck or drake. For Moles (as our Surrey River) work underground, whilst ducks (which Anas doth not) dive under water.'

The only other writer from the reign of Elizabeth (as far as our researches have revealed) who speaks of the Mole was the poet Edmund Spenser. He shows a remarkable knowledge of the rivers of England in Book Four of 'The Faerie Queen'. In the eleventh canto, describing the marriage of Thames and Medway, he writes of

'. . . Mole, that like a nousling Mole doth make

His way still underground, till Thamis he overtake.'

On this same topic of burrowing underground two poets followed Spenser (and possibly Camden). Milton, who wrote of 'sullen Mole that runneth underneath', and Pope, who, in a passage describing Windsor Forest, mentioned 'sullen Mole that hides his diving Flood'.

John Evelyn, the 17th century diarist, who spent the last years of his life at Wotton, on the lower slopes of Leith Hill, scarcely seven miles away from Box Hill, had probably heard of but not investigated the behaviour of the Mole when he wrote about the Rhône and compared the two thus:

'The River Rhône, which parts the city in the midst, dips into a cavern underground about six miles from it and afterwards rises again and runs its open course like our Mole or Swallow near Darking in Surrey.'

Evelyn's great interest was in trees and tree planting. He wrote a book which he called 'Sylva, or a Discourse of Forest Trees' and addressed Charles the Second's newly formed Royal Society on the subject.* In his diary for 27 August 1655 he writes of the trees of Box Hill, as well as returning to the subject of the disappearing

* See Chapter Twelve.

108

Mole, giving us our first word picture of the place.

'Went to Box Hill to see those rare natural bowers, cabinets and shady walk in the Box copses and went to view the Swallow famed for the drying of the River of Darking there, and passing underground at the foot of a huge white cliff or precipice looking westward: the channel where the water sinks in being full of holes: it not rising till some miles distant at Leatherhead. Here we walked to Mickleham and saw Sir F. Stidulph's seat environed with elm trees and walnuts innumerable and of which last he told us they received a considerable revenue. Here are such goodly walks and hills shaded with yew and box as render the place extremely agreeable, it seeming from these evergreens to be summer all the winter for many miles prospect.'

A few years later another diarist, Samuel Pepys, went to Epsom on July 14 1667 on a well-earned holiday from London. He missed by only a few miles the turf and box avenues of Box Hill, but as his experiences are so vividly described and are so typical of both the man and the whole locality, and as they could so easily present an eye-witness account of the hill in 1667, it seems a pity not to quote the relevant passage.

'. . . we took coach and to take the ayre, there being a fine breeze abroad; and I carried them to the well, and there filled some bottles of water (Epsom) to carry home with me; and there I talked with the two women that farm the well, at £12 per annum, of the lord of the manor. (Mr. Evelyn.) . . . Here W. Hewer's horse broke loose, and we had the sport to see him taken again . . . and then I walked them to the wood hard by, and there got them in the thickets till they had lost themselves, and I could not find the way into any of the walks in the wood, which indeed are very pleasant, if I could have found them.

At last got out of the wood again; and I, by leaping down the little bank, coming out of the wood, did sprain my right foot, which brought me great present pain, but presently, with walking it, went away for the present, and so the women and W. Hewer and I walked upon the Downes, where a flock of sheep was; and the most pleasant and innocent sight that ever I saw in my life. We found a shepherd and his little boy reading, far from any houses or sight of people, the Bible to him; so I made the boy read to me, which he did, with the forced tone that children do usually read, that was mighty pretty, and then I did give him something, and went to the father, and talked with him; and I find he had been a servant in my cozen Pepys's house, and told me what was become of their old servants. He did content himself mightily in my liking his boy's reading, and did bless God for him, the most like one of the old patriarchs that ever I saw in my life, and it brought those thoughts of the old age of the world in my mind for two or three days after. We took notice of his woolen knit stockings of two colours mixed, and of his shoes shod with iron, both at the toe and heels, and with great nails in the soles of his feet, which was mighty pretty: and, taking notice of them, why, says the poor man, the downes, you see, are full of stones, and we are faine to shoe ourselves thus; and these, says he, will make the stones fly till they ring before me. I did give the poor man something, for which he was mighty thankful, and I tried to cast stones with his horne crooke. He values his dog mightily, that would turn a sheep any way which he would have him, when he goes to fold them: told me there was about eighteen score sheep in his flock, and that he hath four shillings a week the year round for keeping of them: and Mrs. Turner, in the common fields here, did gather one of the prettiest nosegays that ever I saw in my life. So to our coach . . . and we set out for home . . . in the cool of the evening . . . Anon it grew dark, and we had the pleasure to see several glow-wormes, which was mighty pretty, but my foot begins more and more to pain me, which Mrs. Turner, by keeping her warm hand upon it, did much ease . . .'

Celia Fiennes, who lived from 1662 to 1741, is our next witness to the 'prospects' from and around Box Hill. She was of gentle birth, being related to the famous family of Saye and Sele of Broughton Castle. A singularly 'liberated' woman for her time, she adventured on her own through England, enduring the diabolical roads and inns with the objective interest of the explorer. She had stamina and courage, both physical and moral, surviving an encounter with a footpad and her own temerity in telling the Scots that they were lazy! Her diaries which, like those of Pepys, had not been intended for publication, show that she was as accurate an observer as any writer before Defoe. In them she has left two accounts of Box Hill, one from the tour of 1694, the other about eight or nine years later. Her interests were mainly in Nonconformity and the New Society. Her descriptions were more conventional. Prospects and vistas are 'neat', as favourite a word with her as 'pretty' was with Pepys. In 1694 she wrote, describing Box Hill, ' . . .the hill is full of box which is cut out in several walks, shady and pleasant to walk in tho' the smell is not very agreeable; the brow of the hill being such a

110

height gives a large prospect of a fruitful vale full of inclosures and woods . . .' She then goes on to repeat the story first related by Camden, of the disappearing Mole and the duck which was forced into one of the swallows, though she sensibly concludes ' . . . how they could force the duck into so difficult a way, or whether anything of this is more than conjecture must be left to everyone's liberty to judge!' Compared with her other writings there is little here of the eye-witness and more than a suspicion of listening to gossip — a habit she shared with journalists and historians as eminent as Herodotus!

In her later journals, written between 1701 and 1703, Celia gives us some more information about Box Hill, chiefly as a Playground for the concourses of people who already tended to assemble at Epsom.

'The greatest pleasure of Epsum is either Banstead Downs where is good aire or good rideing for coaches and horses with a pleasant view of the country, or else Box Hill which is six or seven miles off and is the continuation of the ridge of hills I mentioned by Maidstone: it's a great height and shows you a vast precipice down on the farther side and such a vast vale full of woods inclosures and little towns; there is a very good river that runs by a little town called Darken just at the foote of this hill, very famous for good troutts and great store of fish; on this hill the top is covered with box, whence its name proceeds, and there is other wood but it's all cut in long private walks very shady and pleasant and this is a great diversion to the Company, and would be more frequented if nearer Epsom Town.'

An indication of what this great diversion was is contained in the writing of another observer of the period, John Macky, a government spy, like Defoe. During a spell in prison in 1714 he wrote 'A Journey through England — Familiar Letters from a Gentleman Here to his Friend Abroad'. In this he remarks 'It is very easy for Gentlemen and Ladies insensibly to lose their Company in these pretty labyrinths of Box Wood, and divert themselves unperceived . . . and it may justly be called the Palace of Venus.'

Celia Fiennes' eye-witness account of Box Hill was followed, only a few years later, by that of Daniel Defoe, the author of 'Robinson Crusoe'. His book, 'A Tour through the Whole Island of Great Britain', was originally published between 1724 and 1726 by which time he had covered most of the land right up to John O'Groats. He was by this time over sixty and approaching the end of his long and colourful career during which he had been extremely active as reporter, Whig propagandist, Government agent and spy. As a pamphleteer he had met his match only once, in Jonathan Swift. His undoubted ability as a journalist and his flair for describing people and scenes through the eyes of a Nonconformist make his journal akin to that of Celia Fiennes, though his work, unlike hers, *was* intended for publication. To read it is to take a trip through England in the eighteenth century not rivalled again until the time of Arthur Young and William Cobbett.

Defoe, like his predecessors, was intrigued by the publicity given to the swallow-holes on the Mole. He had read of them in Camden's 'Britannia' and had himself lived within a few miles of these marvels. Characteristically, he went to see them for himself and was utterly scathing about the exaggerated accounts given by Camden and his later learned editor, the Bishop of Salisbury.

'Now 'tis something strange,' he wrote, 'for me to take upon me, after two such authorities, to say, that neither of these is right . . . The River Mole passes by Beechworth Castle in a full stream; and for near a mile farther on to the west of the castle, it takes into its stream Darking Brook, as they call it, and has upon it a large corn mill call'd Darking Mill; below this it runs close at the foot of Box Hill, near that part of the hill which is called the Stomacher; then, as if obstructed by the hill, it turns a little south, and runs across the road which leads from Darking to Leatherhead, where it is apparently rapid and strong; and then fetches a circuit round a park, formerly belonging to Sir Richard Studdolph, and which is part of it, within sight of Leatherhead; and so keeps a continued channel to the very town of Leatherhead; so that there is no such thing as a natural bridge, or a river lost, no, not at all; and in the winter, in time of floods the stream will be very large, and rapid all the way above ground, which I affirm of my own knowledge, having seen it so, on many occasions.'

Defoe has already been given the credit due to him as the first writer to demolish the ancient legend, in the chapter on the Mole. He goes on to show that it can be very simply explained. There are several swallows, he pointed out, and not one and went on to explain that the water percolated away in little channels with water in them 'not so big as would fill a pipe of a quarter of an inch diameter.' It 'trills away out of the river and sinks insensibly into the ground . . . these swallows, tho' they diminish the stream much, do not so drink it up as to make it disappear. But that, where it crosses the road near Mickleham, it runs very sharp and broad, nor did I ever know it dry up in the dryest summer in that place, tho' I lived in the neighbourhood several years: on the contrary I have known it so deep, that waggons and carriages have not dar'd to go through . . . This part which I say has the least water, continuing about half a mile, we then perceive the channel insensibly to have more water than before; that is to say, that as it sunk in gradually and insensibly, so it takes vent again in the like manner in thousands of little springs, and unseen places, very few in any quantity, till in another half mile, it is a full river again and passes in full stream under Leatherhead Bridge, as above, and for the truth of this I appeal to the knowledge of the inhabitants of Darking, Mickleham, Leatherhead and all the country round.'

From this accomplished and accurate study of the problem of the swallows Defoe proceeded to deal in detail with the town of Dorking, its principal inhabitants and its market. In passing he mentioned, in a characteristic dry phrase, 'the so much celebrated house of Mr. Evelyn at Wotton, near Darking, not that it is not worth notice, but because so many other writers have said so much of it.'

Later Defoe turned to the matter already touched upon by Macky, thereby parading his non-conformist conscience on an aspect of Box Hill which belongs under the heading Playground rather than Sanctuary.

'On the top of Box Hill and in view of this town (Dorking), grows a very great beech tree, which by way of distinction is call'd 'The Great Beech', and a very great tree it is; but I mention it on the following account, under the shade of this tree was a little vault or cave, and here every Sunday . . . there used to be a rendezvous of coaches and horsemen, with abundance of gentlemen and ladies from Epsome to take the air, and walk in the box woods; and in a word, divert, or debauch, or perhaps both, as they thought fit, and the game encreas'd so much that it began almost on a sudden to make a great noise in the country.

'A vintner who kept the Kings Arms Inn at Darking, taking notice of the constant and unusual flux of company thither, took the hint from the prospect of his advantage, which offer'd, and obtaining leave from Sir Adam Brown, whose manor and land it was, furnish'd this little cellar or vault with tables, chairs, etc., and with wine and eatables to entertain the ladies and gentlemen on Sunday nights, as above; and this was so agreeable to them as that it increased the company exceedingly; in a word by these means, the concourse of gentry, and in consequence of the country people, became so great that the place was like a little fair; so that at length the country began to take notice of it, and it was very offensive, especially to the best governed people; this lasted some years, I think two or three, and tho' complaint was made of it to Sir Adam Brown, and the neighbouring justices, alledging the revelling and the indecent mirth that was among them, and on the Sabbath Day too, yet it did not obtain a suitable redress; whereupon a certain set of young men, of the town of Darking, and perhaps prompted by some others, resenting the thing also, made an unwelcome visit to the place once on a Saturday night, just before the usual time of their wicked mirth, and behold when the coaches and ladies etc from Epsome appear'd the next afternoon, they found the cellar or vault and all that was in it, blown up with gunpowder; and so secret was it kept, that upon the utmost enquiry it cou'd never be heard or found our who were the persons that did it. That action put an end to their revels for a great while; nor was the place ever repair'd that I heard of, at least it was not put to the same wicked use that it was employ'd in before.'

This story is a sharp reminder that even in the eighteenth century the London tourist was not always welcomed by the local people with the same deference the shepherd paid to Pepys. It is typical also of the sort of thing which attracted the attention of the writers of the sixteenth and seventeenth centuries. They were much more concerned with picturesque legends, social problems, commercial values and rich mens' properties than the beauty of the scenery, of which they had little or no appreciation. For example, in the Gentleman's Magazine of 1787 we find Box Hill described as 'a useless waste'! It occurs in an account of the box groves which grew there then as they do today. The writer attributes their existence to the Earl of Arundel and comments 'How few possessors of such useless wastes have left behind them so valuable an example of their patriotic pursuits!' (A correspondent to a later number of the magazine corrected this assertion stating, quite correctly, that 'The Box Trees on Box Hill were there before the Earl of Arundel's time.' He did not, however, take him to task for describing the hill in such disparaging terms.)

Similarly Defoe, commenting on the progress of the Weald from forest to industrial area, is concerned only with the prospect of

114

timber becoming scarcer and therefore dearer, not with the effect on the landscape.

'All on the right-hand, that is to say, south (of Box Hill), is exceedingly grown with timber, has abundance of waste and wild grounds, and forests and woods, with many large iron-works, at which they cast great quantities of iron caldrons, chimney-backs, furnaces, retorts, boiling pots, and all such necessary things of iron; besides iron cannon, bomb-shells, stink-pots, hand-grenadoes, and cannon ball, etc in an infinite quantity, and which turn to very great account; though at the same time the works are prodigiously expensive, and the quantity of wood they consume is exceeding great, which keeps up that complaint . . . that timber would grow scarce, and consequently dear, from the great quantity consum'd in the iron works in Sussex.'

It is to the Gentleman's Magazine that we turn again for a final glimpse of Box Hill in the eighteenth century. An 'Anonymous Visitor'' wrote an account, published in the magazine in 1787, which contains the following description of the hill.

'Soon after passing Juniper Hall, Box Hill is on the left. The first part is fine turf; at the top is a large quantity of that evergreen which also grows on the steep and lofty face of it, overhanging the River Mole, and which is otherwise nothing in that place but bare chalk.' He then goes on to write about the swallows on the river and the gentlemen's houses round about. Beautiful scenery had yet to be invented.

CHAPTER 9
THE LITERARY ASSOCIATIONS OF BOX HILL.
JOHN WESLEY, WILLIAM COBBETT, FANNY BURNEY AND JANE AUSTEN

During the second half of the eighteenth century and the earlier years of the nineteenth, two men possessed of burning enthusiasm, though in very different causes, rode past Box Hill on their various journeys; John Wesley and William Cobbett. John Wesley's Journals contain the story of riding and driving nearly a quarter of a million miles in Britain, preaching and spreading the gospel. He was a man of tremendous energy in the service of Christ and of voracious appetite for the reading of books and the winning of souls. How he contrived to read all he did and ride all the miles that he did is a matter of wonder. Perhaps he read as he jogged along. He had the same introverted disregard of scenery exhibited by St. Bernard of Clairvaulx, who once walked all day by the shores of the Lake of Geneva and saw no lake.

Wesley established a congregation at Dorking by a sermon in the street on January 13th, 1764, and he visited Dorking either from London or from Reigate on fourteen occasions between 1774 and 1790. He always chose to make his visits there in the winter months. In summer he rode further afield. Perhaps this may account in part for his not mentioning the scenery. At his first sermon there were at the outset only two or three little children who were 'the whole of my congregation, but it quickly increased though the air was sharp and the ground exceeding wet. And all behaved well but three or four grumbling men who stood so far off that they disturbed none but themselves.'

By November 1772 Wesley had opened the new 'house' at Dorking and was much comforted thereby. Indeed all went well with the new congregation and in February of 1783 Wesley so far relaxed as to take a walk 'through the lovely gardens of Lord Grimstone.' In February of 1787 he found a 'lively and well established people' and in November of the same year the congregation had become 'large and serious'. But he began to have doubts of them in his old age when his own prodigious strength was failing. On January 25th, 1790, he related:

'I went to Dorking and laboured to awaken a harmless, honest, drowsy people, who for many years have seemed to stand stock still, neither increasing nor decreasing.'

This was his last reference to the Box Hill area. Once indeed he had referred to the gardens, but never to the scenery. Not for him to connect spiritual drowsiness with the warm climate of a town protected from northerly and north-easterly winds by the chalk ridge of Box Hill, and from south-westerly gales by the greensand ridge of Leith Hill, creating a haven where one can grow vines on the southerly side of a house.

William Cobbett was another great traveller on horseback. He had the acute eye of a yeoman farmer for the agriculture and of a radical politician for the commotions of the troubled years following the Napoleonic wars. During the course of his 'Rural Rides' he visited Box Hill, Albury and Reigate. On September 25th, 1822, he wrote: 'This county of Surrey presents to the eye of the traveller a greater contrast than any other county in England. It has some of the very best and some of the worst lands, not only in England, but in the world. For five miles (from Chertsey) on the road towards Guildford the land is a rascally common covered with poor heath, except where the gravel is so near the top as not to suffer even the heath to grow . . . (On Merrow Down) we are here upon a bed of chalk, where the downs always afford good sheep food . . .'

In his diary for September 3rd 1823 Cobbett accurately described the chalk and sand ridges and, as a farmer, appraised the agricultural values of the chalk of the North Downs and the greensand of Leith Hill. He was looking neither for views nor for souls to save, though he did occasionally rejoice when he encountered a profusion of Nonconformists or a scarcity of Anglicans! What he really liked to see were sleek cattle and fine fields of wheat and turnips.

On October 26th, 1826, Cobbett wrote: 'We . . . came through Dorking to Colley Farm, near Reigate, where I slept . . . I desired George,* (at Chilworth,) to look round the country and asked him if he did not think it was very pretty. I put the same question when we got into the beautiful neighbourhood of Dorking . . . From Thursley to Reigate inclusive, on the chalk side as well as the sand side, the crops of turnips, of both kinds, were pretty nearly as good as I ever saw them in my life . . . At Aldbury . . . I saw a piece of cabbages, of the large kind, which will produce, I should think, not much short

* his servant

of five and twenty tons to the acre . . . At Mr Pym's at Colley Farm, we found one of the very finest pieces of mangel wurzel that I had ever seen in my life . . . I have never seen a more beautiful mass of vegetation, and I had the satisfaction to learn, after having admired the crop, that the seed *came from my own shop*, and that it had been *saved by myself!'*

Wesley and Cobbett were men whose sense of mission carried them over the length and breadth of Britain. Their association with Box Hill was a passing one and they left no memorials there of their passing. The ashes of their camp fires have long blown away. If their ghosts walked anywhere, it would certainly not be on Box Hill. With Fanny Burney, of whom we write next, it would be far otherwise.

Until George Meredith came to live permanently in his cottage near Mickleham in Victorian times, Fanny Burney, novelist, diarist and letter-writer, had the greatest opportunity of all the writers associated with Box Hill to absorb the atmosphere of the place. She lived on or near it from 1793, the year of her marriage, until 1802. Even before that she had known the district as a visitor, when staying with her friends, the Locks, at Norbury Park, or with her married sister, Mrs Phillips, at Mickleham Cottage. The seven volumes of her diary and letters are full of comments on the people she encountered, though not on the scenery among which she dwelt. She did not have the eye for nature which Wordsworth and the Romantic School of Lakeland Poets were employing. It would have been remarkable if she had, for she was a child of her age, the age of the formal court and the formal garden, an age when Dr. Johnson (who read and admired her work) could say of the South Downs that they were 'a country so truly desolate that if one had the mind to hang oneself for desperation at being obliged to live there it would be difficult to find a tree on which to fasten the rope!'

Fanny Burney however did most certainly love the locality, and she set up a happy home there after she married. In her letters she referred more than once to its beauty. When she and her husband moved from Phenice Farm, near Polesden Lacy, to a cottage at Bookham, she wrote, 'Our views are not so beautiful as at Phenice Farm'. But she added later, 'We enjoy the beauty of the country around us in long romantic strolls.' Her published works however were typical of the domestic novels popular at the time. It was her acute observation of modes and manners in her three novels

'Evelina', 'Cecilia' and 'Camilla' which brought her her reading public. 'Camilla' is still remembered in the name of the hamlet 'Camilla Lacey' near Box Hill and West Humble Station, though 'Camilla Cottage', her own cottage, was destroyed later by fire.

There was a curious encounter between Sir Walter Scott and Fanny Burney, now Madame D'Arblay, as late as November 18, 1826, which Sir Walter included in his journal:

'Was introduced to Madame D'Arblay, the celebrated authoress of Evelina and Cecilia — an elderly lady with no remains of personal beauty, but with a simple and gentle manner, a pleasing expression of countenance and apparently quick feelings. She told how at Mrs Thrales's Samuel Johnson sat in a kind of reverie and suddenly broke out; 'you should read this new work, Madam, you should read Evelina; everyone says it is excellent, and they are right.' Madame D'Arblay said that when she heard of this she could only give vent to her rapture by dancing and skipping round a mulberry tree in the garden. She was very young at the time. I trust I shall see this lady again.'

There is an echo of this admiration for Fanny Burney from Boswell's Life of Samuel Johnson. Boswell tells of finding Johnson at tea with Fanny Burney on Monday May 26, 1783. 'I mentioned Cecilia. Johnson (with an air of animated satisfaction), 'Sir, if you talk of Cecilia, talk on'.'

Fanny Burney first came to Mickleham when she was recovering from an illness brought on by a trying five years as second Keeper of the Robes to Queen Charlotte, wife of George the Third. Fanny's elder sister, Susannah, was married to a retired Captain of Marines who lived at Mickleham, and Susannah wrote describing the colony of French Emigrés, fugitives from the Terror in Paris, who had established themselves in the village. One group of the Emigrés had taken the tenancy of Juniper Hall, a large and handsome building to which we shall be referring again. There they had established their salon — through the good offices of Mr. Lock — and there they were faintly echoing the brilliant social life they had lived in Paris before the Fall of the Bastille. The great and not yet notorious Talleyrand had visited them there. Resident were Lally Tollendal, the Marquise de La Chàtre, Madame de Staël, and a certain distinguished regular soldier, General D'Arblay, Adjutant General to Lafayette. These had escaped from France with their lives but not their fortunes, to the peace of the Surrey countryside where Mr Lock of Norbury

Park had befriended them. He was a generous patron of art and literature, and as such was also a friend of the Burney family. While touring in southern England in the later stages of her convalescence after her breakdown at Court, Fanny Burney came to stay at Norbury Park and there first met the Emigrés.

The French Emigrés must have been fascinating people to their Norbury Park and Surrey audiences. They had not merely come from the scenes of the dreadful drama of which all Surrey and all England were talking, but they had played major parts in the first act of that drama. The two Burney sisters were attracted like moths to a candle. The brilliance of the conversation at Juniper Hall provided a vivid contrast to Fanny's experience of life at the staid court of George the Third. As Duff Cooper aptly puts it in his 'Life of Talleyrand':

'prim little figures, they had wandered out of the sedate drawing rooms of 'Sense and Sensibility', and were in danger of losing themselves in the alcoves of 'Les Liaisons Dangereuses'.'

Doctor Burney, Fanny's eminent father, warned the sisters of their danger. The French had been living openly with their lovers, as was their habit in Paris, and were puzzled when Fanny's admiration for them cooled rapidly. There was however one of them for whom her regard remained unaltered — General D'Arblay. She was a good judge of character. After knowing him for barely two months, she wrote to her father:

'M. D'Arblay is one of the most singularly interesting characters that can ever have been formed. He has a sincerity, a frankness, an ingenuous openness of nature, that I had been unjust enough to think could not belong to a Frenchman. With all this, which is his military portion, he is passionately fond of literature, a most delicate critic in his own language, well versed in both Italian and German and a very elegant poet. He has just undertaken to become my French master for pronunciation and he gives me long daily lessons in reading. Pray expect wonderful improvements!'

Not perhaps surprisingly, these French lessons which took place mainly at Juniper Hall though sometimes at Mrs. Phillips' cottage, followed the pattern set in Shakespeare's charming love scene between Henry the Fifth and the French Princess, Katherine. In vain did Dr. Burney warn:

'For heaven's sake, my dear Fanny, do not part with your heart too rapidly, or involve yourself in deep engagements which it will be difficult to dissolve; and in the last degree imprudent, as things are at present circumstanced, to fulfil.'

Indeed D'Arblay had already offered Fanny his hand, 'candidly acknowledging the slight hope he entertained of ever recovering the fortune he had lost by the revolution'.

Eventually Dr. Burney gave way and sent his consent to the marriage, though he remained sufficiently disapproving to absent himself from the ceremony in Mickleham Parish Church on 31 July 1793. Eight years of happiness followed in the lovely countryside in which they had first met, for D'Arblay's offer of service in the Toulon Expedition under Lord Hood was mercifully refused, and Fanny had him all to herself until the Truce of Amiens in 1802 made it possible for him to return to France. Fanny loyally went with him and they never returned to Mickleham. The quick collapse of the Truce left Fanny an exile from her native land. For ten years she was stranded in France, cut off from all her English connections. Then in 1812 her husband obtained for her a passage on a ship bound officially for America, but due to make a clandestine call at Dover! 1812 was the year of the outbreak of the Maritime War between England and the United States, and by a chance more suited to a novel than to real history, the ship, on which she and her eighteen year old son Alex were travelling, was taken as a prize by the British Navy. Fanny returned once more to France during the Hundred Days between Elba and Waterloo, but her son Alex wanted to establish himself in England, the land of his birth, so the family returned to England when peace came. They lived in Bath, where General D'Arblay died in 1818.

During her years in France Madame D'Arblay recounts how a chance meeting with Talleyrand recalled many memories of her cottage at Bookham not far from Box Hill. These had been days of unmingled happiness. First the D'Arblays had gone to live at Phenice Farm, which still stands, a square red brick building beside the lane from West Humble to Bookham. It is a lonely place, where yellow-hammers flit before one along the hedges and whitethroats rattle out their husky little songs on summer days — a sharp contrast to the scenes of action of D'Arblay's earlier life. By October they had moved to a little cottage at Great Bookham. Here Alexander had been born, and Fanny's diary is full of motherly delight at the progress of the infant prodigy, and his proud display before Queen Charlotte at Windsor. At Great Bookham Fanny began writing 'Camilla' and D'Arblay began gardening, and they decided to have a

121

cottage built for them at West Humble. Fanny's Journal is full of delightful descriptions of the progress of the cottage, and it must have given her pleasure to turn back to them during her long exile in France.

'The situation of the field (for Camilla Cottage) is remarkably beautiful. It is in the valley between Mr Lock's Park at Norbury and Dorking, where land is so scarce that there is not another possessor within many miles who would part upon any terms with half an acre . . . Imagine but the ecstasy of M. D'Arblay with all in his own way an entirely new garden. He dreams now of cabbage walks and potato beds, bean perfumes and peas blossoms. My mother should send him a little sketch to help in his flower garden.'

Throughout 1796 and 1797 the cottage was being built and a well dug to the depth of a hundred feet — blocked to prevent accidents from and to 'hazardous boys'. The family moved in in November 1797. The spirits of Little Alex were so high on finding two or three rooms

'totally free for his horse (alias any stick he can pick up) and himself, unencumbered by chairs and tables and suchlike lumber, that he was as merry as little Andrew, and as wild as twenty colts.'

While Fanny was absent in 1800 on a visit to the Queen at Greenwich things went wrong in Camilla Cottage garden. Truth to tell D'Arblay was a better soldier than a gardener, inclined to pull up asparagus in mistake for weeds. Fanny wrote on her return:

'The horses of a neighbouring farmer broke through our hedges, and have made a kind of bog of our meadow, by scampering in it during the wet; the sheep followed who have eaten up all our greens, every sprout and cabbage and lettuce, destined for the winter;while the horses dug up our turnips and carrots; and the swine, pursuing such examples, have trod down all the young plants, besides devouring whatever the others left of vegetables. Our potatoes, left from our abrupt departure, in the ground, are all rotten and frost-bitten and utterly spoilt; and not a single thing has our whole ground produced for us since we came home'.

This was in the early months of 1800, but by April Fanny was describing the dearth, which was one of the factors that drove both France and England to sign the Treaty of Amiens.

'The poor people about us complain that they are nearly starved, and the children of the journeymen of the tradesmen of Dorking

come to our door to beg halfpence for a little bread.'
She blamed both bad harvests and the Income Tax! Naturally enough
the scenery around — its beauty and its wide views — escape the
pen of Fanny, more closely interested in her family and in the hard-
ships of the people. The immediate background, the cottage in which
she lived, has gone, but there is still Juniper Hall to remind us of
her. Its outward appearance has been considerably altered since
1793. Situated in the angle between Mickleham Road and Headley
Lane, it immediately attracts the eye as one comes over the brow
from Burford Bridge. The warm red brick and large windows of the
front of the house, seen beyond the dark spreading branches of the
big cedars on the lawn, offer a friendly welcome, but they are
later than Fanny's time, and only inside the house in the drawing
room and hall would she have felt at home. This south-facing front,
with its pointed gables and tall chimneys, is well-proportioned and
sits snugly beneath the shelter of the steep, tree-clad slope of White
Hill. On the Headley Lane side one is more aware of the size of the
place. It dominates the lane as a ship dominates its quayside moor-
ings, a great hulk of a building, long and narrow. Originally it had
been an inn, the Royal Oak. In 1772 it had been bought, along with
sixty acres of surrounding land, by Sir Cecil Bishopp, who had
originally intended to pull it down and build a new house there.
However, he changed his mind, deciding to add further rooms to
the nucleus of the inn building. He turned the sixty acres into a
park. Like many of his age he was a great planter of trees, and we
owe to him part of the graceful beauty of the tree-clad landscape in
which Juniper Hall stands today. From Bishopp the Hall passed to
Jenkinson — 'an affluent lottery-house keeper', who rented the Hall
to the Emigrés. It now belongs to the National Trust, from whom it
is rented by the Field Studies Council, an educational trust which
provides courses in practical fieldwork, chiefly for geographers
and biologists, from schools and universities.

The interior of Juniper Hall has been altered to provide class-
rooms, laboratories and dormitories, but it has been altered with
care and taste so that the house loses little of its character, in particular the graceful winding staircase beneath its glass dome, and the
lovely drawing room, decorated with gilded plaster work in the Adam
style. At least the Emigrés would recognise these. During the
evenings Juniper Hall is noisy with the chatter and scamperings of
students; but during the day, when the last excited talkative party,

complete with its maps, collecting gear and packed lunches, has scrunched away down the gravelled drive, silence descends softly on the building. It is then, if ghosts exist, not at midnight, that they emerge quietly from the shadows, glancing in interested perplexity at the notebooks of the students littering the tables in the drawing room, peeping through the windows at the wagtails running on the lawn beneath the cedars — friendly harmless ghosts, who loved this place, and in their day were happy there.

The career of Fanny Burney as a novelist reached its limit with the writing of 'Camilla'. It coincided with the first ventures in authorship of another lady novelist, who wrote in the same vein as Fanny, but was destined to become an incomparably greater writer. This was Jane Austen.

Jane Austen was eighteen when 'Camilla' was published. It is possible Jane may have seen, or even met, Fanny Burney. Jane's god-parents lived in Great Bookham, and she visited them from time to time. Jane seems to have been an admirer of Fanny, for Jane's name appears on the subscription list to 'Camilla'. What is more, the title of her most famous novel 'Pride and Prejudice' may have been taken from the last paragraph of 'Camilla', where these words appear, three times repeated, in capital letters.

Jane laid the scene of one of her novels, 'Emma', published in 1816, in Surrey. One famous episode of it actually takes place on Box Hill. 'Emma' is a charming and witty account of the life and sensibilities of the ruling classes of Surrey, set in and around a small town called Highbury, which some have identified with Leatherhead. Box Hill is selected by the heroine of the story, Emma Woodhouse, as the venue for a picnic. Was there an echo of a curiosity Jane herself had felt when she wrote: 'Emma had never been to Box Hill; she wished to see what everybody found so much worth seeing'? There is however very little in the way of a description of the countryside in the chapter where the picnic episode takes place:

'Seven miles were travelled in expectation of enjoyment, and everybody had a burst of admiration on first arriving; but in the general amount of the day there was a deficiency. There was a langour, a want of spirits, a want of union, which could not be got over. They separated too much into parties. The Eltons walked together; Mr. Knightley took charge of Miss Bates and Jane; and Emma and Harriet belonged to Frank Churchill . . .

In the judgement of most people looking on it must have had such appearance as no English word but flirtation could very well describe. 'Mr Frank Churchill and Miss Woodhouse flirted excessively' — they were laying themselves open to that very phrase . . . ''I say nothing of which I am ashamed'', said Churchill with lively impudence, ''I saw you first in February. Let everybody on the hill hear me if they can. Let my accents swell to Mickleham on the one side and to Dorking on the other. I saw you first in February'', and then, whispering, ''Our companions are excessively stupid. What shall we do to rouse them? Any nonsense will serve. They *shall* talk. Ladies and geltlemen, I am ordered by Miss Woodhouse (who, wherever she is, presides) to say that she desires to know what you are thinking of.'' Some laughed and answered good humouredly. Miss Bates said a great deal; Mrs Elton swelled at the idea of Miss Woodhouse presiding; Mr Knightley's answer was the most distinct:'Is Miss Woodhouse sure that she would like to hear what we are all thinking of?''

''Oh, no, no, no — '' cried Emma, laughing as carelessly as she could — ''upon no account in the world. It is the very last thing I would stand the brunt of just now. Let me hear anything rather than what you are all thinking of!''

And so Jane Austen's picnic goes on with its chatter. They are even threatened with turns in repeating 'one thing clever, or two things moderately clever, or three things very dull indeed' — the choice of the third being made by Miss Bates, whom Emma insults, for which she is rebuked by Mr. Knightley. By the end of the picnic they are all bored. They have paid no attention to the scenery and are becoming tired of one another's company.

'. . . even Emma grew tired at last of flattery and merriment, and wished herself walking quietly about with any of the others, or sitting almost alone and quite unattended to, in tranquil observation of the beautiful views beneath her . . . The appearance of the servants looking out for them to give notice of the carriages was a joyful sight; and even the bustle of collecting and preparing to depart, and the solicitude of Mrs Elton to have *her* carriage first, were gladly endured in the prospect of the quiet drive home which was to close the very questionable enjoyments of this day of pleasure. Such another scheme, composed of so many ill-assorted people, she hoped never to be betrayed into again.'

So the picnic was a failure. To Emma the day was 'more to be abhorred in recollection than any she had ever passed'. It is an important part of the action of the story, and there is no place in it for descriptions of scenery. Emma was not allowed to escape her noisy companions to contemplate the view from the crest of the escarpment, so there is no account of how it must have looked to Jane in the early years of the nineteenth century; but there is, in the earlier chapters of 'Emma' a description of the view from Donwell Abbey, the home of Mr Knightley, whom Emma eventually was to marry.

'The considerable slope, at nearly the foot of which the Abbey stood, gradually acquired a steeper form beyond its grounds; and at half a mile distant was a bank of considerable abruptness and grandeur, well clothed with wood; and at the bottom of this bank, favourably placed and sheltered, rose the Abbey Mill Farm, with meadows in front, and the river making a close and handsome curve around it.'

This could well have been a description of Priory Farm, beside the Mole, seen from the slopes of Norbury — a view which Jane would see on a drive from Great Bookham. Wherever this glimpse was, this tranquil and beautiful scene had clearly made a great appeal to Jane's sensitive imagination, for she continues:

'It was a sweet view — sweet to the eye and mind; English verdure, English culture, English comfort, seen under a sun bright without being oppressive.'

Was this view far from Box Hill? Did the eyes of Jane Austen rest with pleasure on one of the most beautiful landscapes in the Surrey countryside?

CHAPTER TEN
THE LITERARY ASSOCIATIONS OF BOX HILL
THE AGE OF THE ROMANTICS. KEATS, STEVENSON
AND MEREDITH

In the nineteenth century two outstanding writers and poets, John Keats and George Meredith, knew Box Hill. The former was a passer-by, though he admitted in the letter quoted below that he was influenced by the Hill in his writing of the fourth book of "Endymion". The latter lived on Box Hill for many years.

There were, of course, many other literary visitors, and when one adds their names to those mentioned in the three previous chapters, possibly no other area in Britain save Fleet Street, comparable in size to the triangle of land between Mickleham, Dorking and Ranmore, is associated with so many literary figures.

Hazlitt and Robert Louis Stevenson stayed at the Burford Bridge Hotel. Disraeli wrote "Coningsby" during a long stay at Deepdene near Dorking. Malthus, the economist, lived at Westcott. Richard Sharp, a Whig politician and man-about-town, had his country house at Fredley Farm opposite Juniper Hall. His two nicknames, "The Bishop of Mickleham", and "Conversation Sharp" give clues to the manner of man he was. Sharp entertained a long succession of famous visitors, amongst them Wordsworth, Coleridge, Sir Walter Scott, Campbell, Southey, Moore, Lawrence, Macaulay, J.S. Mill, Huskisson and Lord John Russell. Later in the century Meredith's visitors included R.L. Stevenson, J.M. Barrie, Thomas Hardy, Swinburne, Alice Meynell, and Macaulay's grandson, the young G.M. Trevelyan. From such an assemblage of writers at least two or three loved wild scenery, and might have left a description of Box Hill as it appeared to them in their day — some word picture as detailed and beautiful as the oil painting by John Brett, which serves as our frontispiece. But nowhere have we found such a passage. Apart from Meredith's work, one can gather less from them than from scrutinising the sheet of the One Inch Ordnance Survey map of Dorking, the first edition of which was published in 1816 by Colonel Mudge from his office in the Tower of London. Sharp's visitors were great talkers; Meredith's visitors were pilgrims to Meredith rather than pilgrims to Box Hill.

John Keats visited Box Hill in November 1817 when he was finishing his long poem "Endymion". He stayed at the "Fox and

Hounds", now the Burford Bridge Hotel, and although his stay was short, and November is hardly the best month for the Hill, his perceptiveness of the details of nature brought him closer to what we find most delightful in Box Hill than any of his predecessors.

"Endymion" was a poem he had begun in the Isle of Wight, and he had continued it at Oxford, Stratford on Avon and Hampstead, so it cannot be claimed that Box Hill was the main source of inspiration for the scenery which forms the background to the poem. In earlier parts he had described with delight the sound of "a bee bustling down in the bluebells" and of a "wren light rustling among sere leaves and twigs" and of the sound of "a little breeze to creep between the fans of careless butterflies". Such are not a monopoly of Box Hill, but such it needs a poet's eye and ear to notice, and such a poet was Keats.

Keats alluded to this Box Hill visit in a letter written to his friend Reynolds on November 22 1817:-

"I like this place very much. There is a hill and a dale and a little river. I went up Box Hill this evening after the Moon." He continues in a passage envying Shakespeare for his ability in "Venus and Adonis" to describe a snail pulling in his horns — "Shakespeare has left nothing to say about anything!"

. In Book Four of Endymion is the passage most suggestive of Box Hill:

"Where shall our dwelling be? Under the brow
Of some steep mossy hill, where ivy dun
Would hide us up, although spring leaves were none;
And where dark yew-trees, as we rustle through,
Will drop their scarlet-berry cups of dew!
Oh thou wouldst joy to live in such a place!
Dusk for our loves, yet light enough to grace
Those gentle limbs on mossy beds reclin'd:
For by one step the blue sky shouldst thou find,
And by another, in deep dell below,
See, through the trees, a little river go
All in its midday gold and glimmering . . .

. . .They were perforce content
To sit beneath a fair lone beechen tree;
Nor at each other gaz'd, but heavily
Por'd on its hazel cirque of shedded leaves."

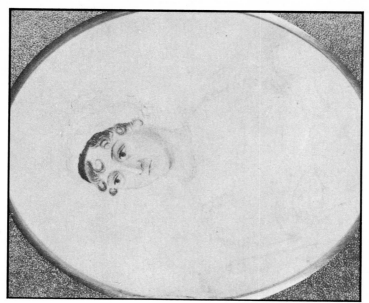

Jane Austen.

Fanny Burney.

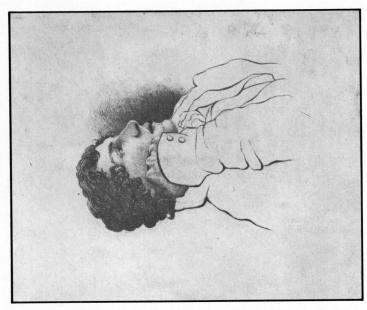

John Keats.

George Meredith.

Polesden Lacy.   *above:* The house. *below:* The terrace.

above: The Military Road, leading originally to the fort on Box Hill, is rich in birds and flowers. *below:* The entrance to the Mole gap. The Roman Stane Street crossed the fields on the left of the picture.

Two views showing the richly wooded landscape of Box Hill.
above: The beech hanger opposite Juniper Hall.
below: The prospect towards Headley seen from Juniper Top.

Alders by the Mole in winter.

Birches in Ashurst Rough.

Beech woodland in Ashurst Rough.
above: Summer. *below:* Winter.

The beech hanger opposite Juniper Hall.

Grove of lime trees near Swanworth Farm.

All of which can scarcely be bettered as a description of Box Hill and the Mole in November.

Robert Louis Stevenson, author of "Kidnapped" and "Treasure Island", of "Travels with a Donkey" and "Weir of Hermiston", might have rivalled the poets with his careful descriptive prose. The Headley Valley and the Mole Gap would have had for him some of the wildness which he described in the Cévennes and in Mull. Stevenson came both to Burford Bridge and to Meredith's House, and he wrote the following account in "Memories and Portraits" of a novel he proposed writing but never wrote (possibly it would have been a sequel to the series "Kidnapped" and "Catriona"), about the Burford Bridge Hotel. The Hotel has been vastly enlarged since his day, but it has the same delightful situation, if not the same air of mystery. This passage was written by R.L.S. some time soon after 1881:-

"There is a fitness in events and places. The sight of a pleasant arbour puts it in our mind to sit there. One place suggests work, another idleness, a third early rising and long rambles in the dew . . . Some places speak distinctly. Certain dank gardens cry aloud for a murder; certain old houses demand to be haunted; certain coasts are set apart for a shipwreck. Other spots again seem to abide their destiny, suggestive and impenetrable, 'miching mallecho'. The inn at Burford Bridge, with its arbours and green garden and silent eddying river — though it is known already as the place where Keats wrote some of his Endymion and Nelson parted from his Emma — still seems to wait the coming of the appropriate legend. Within these ivied walls, behind those old green shutters, some further business smoulders, waiting for its hour. The old Hawes Inn at Queensferry makes a similar call on my fancy . . .

To how many places have we not drawn near with express intimations — 'Here my destiny awaits me'? and we have but dined there and passed on: I have lived both at the Hawes and at the Burford Bridge in a perpetual flutter, on the heels as it seemed of an adventure that should justify the place; but though the feeling had me to bed at night and called me again at morning in one unbroken round of pleasure and suspense, nothing befell me at either worthy of remark. The man or the hour had not yet come; but some day, I think, a boat shall put off from Queensferry, fraught with a dear cargo, and some frosty night a horseman, on tragic errand, shall rattle with his whip upon the green shutters of the inn at Burford. Since the above was first written, I have tried to launch the boat with my own hands in 'Kidnapped'. Some day, perhaps, I may try a rattle at the shutters of Burford Bridge.''

Alas, that day never came. The nearest to rattling the shutters of the Burford Bridge in moments of high drama came from the fists of thirsty travellers and, sixty years after Stevenson stayed there, the reverberation of exploding ''doodle-bugs'' on the crest of the Downs. Perhaps some future writer may yet find inspiration in latent romance, but since Stevenson's day, the inn has changed into a hotel with ballroom and swimming bath. The sense of brooding drama has fled with the oil lamps and the horses.

Of all the poets, diarists and novelists who lived near or came to visit Box Hill, George Meredith, poet and author of ''Diana of the Crossways'' and other novels, was the one whose work owed most to the inspiration of its beauty. He was a naturalist, a lover of country things and a vigorous walker who rambled many miles over the Surrey countryside. He lived for more than twenty years in the cottage he owned at the entrance to the ''Zig-Zag'' valley. He might well, as Edward Thomas suggested, be called a poet for Londoners, a townsman-naturalist, who escaped from the smoke of London at first only on Sunday expeditions, then as a permanent resident.

Meredith's Flint Cottage is famous. Together with the little chalet or summerhouse which he built as his study in the sloping garden behind the cottage, it has changed little. You pass it on your left on your way up the ''Zig-Zag''; you return past it on your way home to the station as you descend the ''Military Road''. The slopes opposite his front door have wild orchids and the trees surrounding it echo with bird song in season. There were nearly always bullfinches there. We wondered whether they were there in Meredith's day. We had a fellow-feeling for Meredith, not because we then admired his novels or his poetry, but because, like us, he became fonder and fonder of Box Hill, and we envied him his permanent home there. Meredith lived at Flint Cottage for the latter part of his life and died there in 1909 at the age of 81. There may be people alive now who are old enough to remember him in his old age, sitting in his bath chair, from which he could see his beloved North Downs. Earlier in his life he had been a man of great physical energy, lean and hard, an athlete among poets. At the age of 61 he was fit enough to join the ''Order of Sunday Tramps'', an early rambling club containing such celebrated alpinists, explorers and scholars as Leslie Stephen,

Douglas Freshfield and F.W. Maitland. Even at this age he was capable of 25 miles of downland. When he was in company he was a walker who talked. Likewise the heroes in his novels are often good walkers and good talkers!

Meredith, writing about his home, Flint Cottage, says:

"I work and sleep in my cottage at present, and anything grander than the days and nights in my porch you will not find away from the Alps: for the dark line of my hill runs up to the stars, the valley below is a soundless gulf. There I pace like a shipman before turning in. In the day with the south west blowing I have a brilliant universe rolling up to me."

This mention of the Alps is the clue to the change in people's taste in scenery, from the love of the formal, ordered landscape to the love of wilderness for its own sake. It had begun with Wordsworth and some of the other Lakeland poets. It had blossomed into a hunger to climb the Alpine peaks and see the ridges run up to the sky, as well as to wander among the gentians in the meadows. The Scottish Highlands, and indeed even the smaller hills and downs of southern Britain could feed this hunger too. A love of downland was in the blood of Meredith. He found it in Box Hill. He wrote of it in "Diana of the Crossways":-

"Through an old gravel cutting a gateway led to the turf of the down, springy turf, bordered on a long line, clear as a race-course, by golden gorse covers, and leftward over the gorse the dark ridge of the fir and heath country ran companionably to the south west, the valley between, with undulations of wood and meadow sunned or shaded, clumps and mounds, promontories, away to the broad spaces of tillage banked by wooded hills, and dimmer beyond and farther, the faintest shadowiness of heights, as a veil to the illimitable. Yews, junipers, radiant beeches, and gleams of service-tree or the whitebeam, spotted the semicircle of swelling green down black and silver."

Many of his novels are set in this type of countryside, but Meredith comes nearest to capturing the spirit of Box Hill itself in a poem "Love in the Valley", which he had written as early as 1851 when he was living at Weybridge. The detail is so accurate that it might be a description of Juniper Top as we knew it in our day.

The poem is a love poem, as the title suggests, and in these extracts Meredith is describing his loved one:

139

"Shy as the squirrel and wayward as the swallow,
Swift as the swallow along the river's light,
Circleting the surface to meet his mirrored winglets,
Fleeter she seems in her stay than in her flight.
Shy as the squirrel that leaps among the pine-tops,
Wayward as the swallow overhead at set of sun,
She whom I love is hard to catch and conquer,
Hard but O the glory of the winning were she won!

Lovely are the curves of the white owl sweeping,
Wavy in the dusk lit by one large star.
Lone on the fir-branch, his rattle-note unvaried,
Brooding o'er the gloom, spins the brown eve-jar.
Darker grows the valley, more and more forgetting,
So were it with me if forgetting could be willed.
Tell the grassy hollow that holds the bubbling well-spring,
Tell it to forget the source that keeps it filled.

Stepping down the hill with her fair companions,
Arm in arm, all against the raying West.
Boldly she sings, to the merry tune she marches,
Brave in her shape, and sweeter unpossessed.
Sweeter — for she is what my heart first awaking
Whispered the world was: morning light is she.
Love that so desires would fain keep her changeless:
Fain would fling the net, and fain would have her free.

Prim little scholars are the flowers in her garden,
Trained to stand in rows, and asking if they please.
I might love them well but for loving more the wild ones:
O my wild ones, they tell me more than these.
You, my wild one, you tell of honied field-rose,
Violet, blushing eglantine in life; and even as they,
They by the wayside are earnest of your goodness,
You are of life's, on the banks that line the way.

Yellow with birdfoot-trefoil are the grass-glades;
Yellow with cinquefoil of the dew-gray leaf;
Yellow with stonecrop; the moss-mounds are yellow;
Blue-necked the wheat sways, yellowing to the sheaf.
Green-yellow, bursts from the copse the laughing yaffle;
Sharp as a sickle is the edge of shade and shine;
Earth in her heart laughs looking at the heavens,
Thinking of the harvest: I look and think of mine.

Could I find a place to be alone with heaven,
I would speak my heart out: heaven is my need.
Every woodland tree is flushing like the dogwood,
Flashing like the whitebeam, swaying like the reed.
Flushing like the dogwood crimson in October;
Streaming like the flag-reed south-west blown;
Flashing as in gusts the sudden-lighted white beam;
All seem to know what is for heaven alone.''

These verses, only a few in a much longer poem, breathe the very spirit of Juniper Top, the place we loved best on Box Hill.

Meredith wrote in one of his letters, "I am, every morning, at the top of Box Hill.'' He must often have gone further, to Juniper Top. This is a vision as a young and vigorous man sees it, or even as an older man might, freed temporarily from his stiffness by striding across the springy turf. This is how we saw Juniper Top on those evening tramps away from London, bright with birdsfoot trefoil, the cinquefoils and stonecrop, among the thyme and wild mignonette at midsummer. We crossed it in May when the whitebeam flashed silver and the wheatfields were blue-green on the upper slopes of the Headley Valley. We saw it too in October when the dogwood flushed red. We saw it on summer evenings when the edge of shade and shine cut "sharp as a sickle'', where the dark of the yew forest fell upon the brilliantly lighted grass, and later as the warm dusk closed in and the nightjar began to spin his "rattle note unvaried''. Only once did we see there "the white owl sweeping''. The white owls (barn owls) are gone now, victims of a technological progress Meredith would surely sometimes have regretted; but the green woodpeckers (yaffles) are still there. Often as we emerged from the trees on Ashurst Rough one would burst from the flanking thickets of Juniper Top and fly laughing in undulating flight, down to the haven of beeches in the valley, just as they had done for Meredith.

Jane Austen peopled Box Hill with her sensitively drawn characters, Fanny Burney loved its beauty but tells us little of it, Wesley and Cobbett were too preoccupied to do so. Keats chose a moonlit November evening; but Meredith was there all the year round. Of all the writers who knew Box Hill he reflected its wild loveliness best. He saw it all and loved it until he became part of it. A contemporary wrote of him that he seemed to have in him "much of the temperament of the fawn'' and that he was "a child of nature who must always be young''. After his death Sir James Barrie wrote a fanciful little essay in which he imagined Meredith sitting on the crest of the hill which rises in front of Flint Cottage, chuckling at the sight of his own funeral cortège solemnly accompanying an empty coffin to the cemetery at Dorking. Meredith's zest for life and delight in loveliness make this idea less fantastic than many of Barrie's fancies. The loveliness is still there for the poet, and for ''the parties stepping down the hill with their fair companions'' to behold and enjoy.

CHAPTER ELEVEN
BOX HILL IN HISTORY

To avoid possible misunderstanding or disappointment it should be said at once that Box Hill is singularly devoid of historical associations of a conventional nature as far as we know. No battles have been fought on or beneath its slopes, no gatherings of mailed barons have assembled there with stern purpose, no rebel hordes have poured through the Mole Gap on their way to sack London. There is not even the ruin of an ancient castle to bear witness to feuds of long ago (though there is a not-so-old fort of which more will be said later). It has been written "Happy is the country which has no history". The phrase could well be applied to Box Hill. It is a serene place, unhaunted by memories of violence, bloodshed or the inhumanity of man to man. Rather has it been, since Roman times, a place where men may find content and peace of mind, a haven for the afflicted, as the Emigrés, the fugitives from Revolutionary France, found it to be. Yet there is the stuff of history here and much of the story of the British people may be read from such mute memorials as the roads and tracks which cross or pass by the hill.

The oldest of these, the track which follows the escarpment of the North Downs and crosses the southern face of Box Hill, has a mediaeval name of modern origin. Owing to the influence of an officer of the Ordnance Survey Department, Captain James, whose work was carried out in the middle years of the nineteenth century, it has become known as the Pilgrims' Way, the supposed route taken by pilgrims journeying to visit the tomb of Thomas A'Becket at Canterbury. But the track is much older than the murder of the Archbishop in 1170. In any case neither Henry the Second himself nor any of Chaucer's later pilgrims went to the shrine at Canterbury from Winchester, a route which might have led them onto this downland track. They went from Southwark, along Watling Street via Rochester, on the five day journey described in the Canterbury Tales. Travellers were moving along the Pilgrims' Way thousands of years before Chaucer's party took the North Kent route in the April showers of 1386.

These travellers were men of the New Stone Age. The track was beaten out in Neolithic times by the feet of these ancient people loping along the natural route of the North Downs from Salisbury Plain to the Straits of Dover, carrying arrowheads and axes made from Wiltshire flint to exchange for salt on the Channel coast. They followed the line of the escarpment for several reasons. Chalk downland drains quickly after rain, a process aided by the steepness of the scarp, so the track was passable in all weathers. The North and South Downs describe wide arcs which enclosed, in ancient times, the impenetrable and dangerous forest which filled the Weald. (The word is the same as the German 'wald", a forest, though it also appears as 'wild' on some old Sussex maps.) The comparatively open slopes of the downs provided the means by which this woodland fastness could be avoided. The track is not invariably a ridgeway, following the crest of the scarp, as the chalk here is frequently overlaid by Clay-with-Flints, as explained in the chapter on geology. This, like the clay of the Weald, was also forested and to be avoided. Thus the track is often a terrace, some way below the crest of the scarp and not far above the line of springs which emerge near the bottom of the slope, providing water for the travellers.

Nowadays the Pilgrims' Way is sometimes part of a metalled road, sometimes a bridle way, sometimes just a footpath. In places there is no preserved route. In others there are obstacles as widely different as thorn scrub (since the partial disappearance of the rabbits), electric fences or even untethered bulls. The 141-mile long path, running mostly on the crest of the downs from Farnham to Dover, approved in July 1969 by what is now the Ministry of the Environment, often coincides with the Pilgrims' Way.

The problem of filling in the gaps in the line of this old track has fascinated many people. Perhaps the best known of these is Hilaire Belloc who wrote about them in his book "The Old Road", published originally in 1904. The red-ink route shown on the map in the book, was arrived at by methods of which the following extract provides an example. Belloc had reached Denbies, overlooking the Mole Gap from the west, towards dusk, on his way eastwards.

"The advancing darkness which we faced restored the conditions of an older time; the staring houses merged with the natural trees; the great empty sky and a river mist gave the illusion of a place unoccupied. It was possible to see the passage of the Mole as those rare men saw it who first worked their way eastwards to the Straits, and had not the suggestion seemed too fantastic for a sober journey of research, one might have taken the appeal of the hills for a kind of guide; imagining that with such a goal the trail would plunge straight across the valley floor to reach it.

By more trustworthy methods, the track of the Old Road was, as I have said, less ascertainable. Presumably it followed, down the shoulder of the hill, a spur leading to the river, but the actual mark of the road was lost, its alignment soon reached ploughed land; nothing of the place of crossing could be determined till the stream itself was examined, nor indeed could we make sure of the true point until we found ourselves unexpectedly aided by the direction of the road when we recovered it upon the further bank. This we left for the dawn of the next day; and so went down into Dorking to sleep.

I have said that from Denbies, or rather from the pits of Dorking Lime Works, the path is apparently lost. It reappears, clearly enough marked, along the lower slope of Box Hill, following the 300-feet contour line; but between the two points is a gap extending nearly a mile on one side of the river and almost half a mile upon the other.''

Belloc contrives to fill in this gap by reasoning. The path which turns north over Ranmore Common must be either an offshoot from the Way or a feeder from the Thames valley. That which leads to Burford Bridge can be no older than the bridge itself. The correct line must therefore be to the point where the stepping stones are now situated. In support of Belloc's theory it may be mentioned that the name of the deserted garden on the east side of the stepping stones (the stones themselves, not the inn!), is the Waypole or Weypole. The ''Gentleman's Magazine'' of 1763 refers to this place as the Way Pole. Such a pole might well have marked the Way where the Mole could be forded.

Belloc continues:

"When we had arrived at this decision in the first hour of day-light we turned eastward, and pursued our way by the raised and yew-lined track which was now quite unmistakable, and which we could follow for a considerable time without hesitation. It ran straight along the 300-feet contour line, and took the southern edge of a wood called Brockham Warren.

Here for a short way we went through a stately but abandoned avenue, with the climbing woods up steep upon our left, and on our right a little belt of cover, through which the fall of the slope below us and the more distant Weald and sandy hills could be seen in happy glimpses. When we came out upon the further side and found the open Down again we had doubled (as it were) the Cape of Boxhill, and found ourselves in a new division of the road.''

This part of the Pilgrims' Way must be familiar to many of the thousands of people who flock to the crest of Box Hill though not all of them may recognise it for what it is. We knew it well and have often followed it on our evening walks, watching the birds in the hedges which bound the fields of Box Hill Farm, searching for the little ladies' tresses orchids in September, or just delighting, as Belloc had done, in the wide prospect of the Weald. It is a lovely place, possessed of great atmosphere derived perhaps from a sense of ancient things which have endured for many centuries.

The other old road which belongs in part to Box Hill was built by the conquering Romans. It is the paved route which they laid through the forest of the Weald, a ruler's edge of a road, constructed by men who, without benefit of bull-dozer or earth-scraper, chain-saw or dynamite, nevertheless overcame such obstacles as swamp and primeval oak woodland in a manner not to be equalled again until some 17 or 18 centuries later. Originally the road was made to link the territory of the pro-Roman British chief or minor king, Cogidubnus, with London. Cogidubnus ruled over the people who lived around modern Chichester which the Romans called Novio-magus Regnensium, the New Market of the Regni, Cogidubnus' subjects. When the Romans first landed in Britain, under both Julius Caesar and Claudius, they came by the short cross-Channel route to Pevensey, and Richborough, near Sandwich. Thence they fought their way to Londinium by way of Canterbury and Rochester, along the line which was later to be that of Watling Street. However the alliance with Cogidubnus enabled them to develop an important port at Fishbourne, then a deep-water harbour, near Chichester. This necessitated the construction of the road to London. The Saxons, marvelling at it, called it the Stone, or Stane, Street, and that remains its name today. It is interesting that the name of this, the younger route, goes back further than the nineteenth century map-maker's name for the much older Neolithic track, the Pilgrims' Way.

Stane Street seems never to have had much military importance. It was first an Imperial posting route, later more of a commercial road by which corn and other commodities were brought to London from the rich farmlands of the Sussex coastal plain, together with the imports of Fishbourne. From Chichester it ran by Pulborough, Billingshurst, Ockley, Dorking, Epsom, Ewell and Merton, to the Thames at Southwark.

Box Hill overlooks the line of Stane Street, which comes over the eastern slopes of Leith Hill, through Redlands Wood, runs through Dorking (part of it is said to have been uncovered in Dorking churchyard) and crosses the fields of Bradley Farm, below Ranmore, on its way to the crossing of the Mole. This was somewhere near Burford Bridge. From the river its course lies up the rising ground, through Fredley, past Juniper Hall, then up the side of White Hill and on to Ewell. Belloc states that a portion of the road was uncovered when the lawn was laid at Juniper Hall. When the dual carriage-way between Dorking and Leatherhead was being constructed, just before the Second World War, the place where Stane Street crossed the Mole was established. It was traced on both sides of the river and the conclusion was reached that it forded rather than bridged the Mole as had previously been supposed. Once the steep slope of Juniper Hill at the western end of White Hill has been surmounted, it turns sharply in the direction of London along the line of the track called Downs Road and so passes out of the sight of Box Hill.

For 400 years, a stretch of time equal to that between the reigns of Elizabeth the First and Elizabeth the Second, the traffic of Imperial Rome moved along this road beneath the Whites and the long slope of the Downs rising to the crest of Box Hill. It was a peaceful route, used more by civilian officials and wagon-loads of merchandise than by the Army. It probably saw few legionaries. Winbolt wrote "apart from very small detachments of a semi-military police, stationed at the four 'mansiones' (posting stations) to keep order on the road, soldiers were probably never seen on Stane Street". It is interesting to speculate whether the men detailed to serve at these posts considered themselves lucky to be given what was probably, in modern soldiers' parlance, "a cushy job", when they might easily have been posted to the Wall, or if they were bored by what must have been a fairly uneventful life.

After the Romans came the Saxons. Their line of advance in the country below Box Hill reverted to that of the pre-historic Pilgrims' Way, running east to west along the line of the Downs though probably at the foot of the scarp rather than the crest. The Saxons followed river valleys and lowlands where they could. It is significant that the High Street in Dorking, a Saxon town, runs east-west, across the line of the Roman road. Like their long distant Neolithic predecessors, the Saxons avoided the Weald, the great forest of

147

Anderida as the Romans had called it, until pressure of population in later years forced them to begin clearing it. They let the metalled road they called the Stane or Stone Street sink slowly into the Wealden clay. As with most Roman constructions they regarded it with a mixture of awe and fear, regarding it as the work of giants or devils. In any case they lacked the technical ability to keep it in repair even if they had wanted to do so.

Throughout the Middle Ages the east-west route remained more important than the north-south one. This is indicated by the siting of castles in the river gaps through the Downs. These castles were built there, not so much to guard the river gaps themselves as the crossing places of the rivers which travellers along the downland route had to descend from to negotiate. The little chapel at West Humble, now a ruin, may well have been placed there for these travellers to pray for a safe crossing of the river or to offer thanks for having safely got across. Guildford Castle guarded the crossing of the Wey; Rochester Castle that of the Medway. The little river Darent had a whole string of castles along its valley, at Otford, Shoreham, Eynsford, Farningham and Horton Kirby. It is odd that no such fortification appears to have existed in the valley of the Mole. The obvious explanation is that no castle was built beneath Box Hill simply because it was not needed. Linear defence against a foe coming from the south — from Gaul, from France, or from a Roman-occupied Gaul or a German-occupied France — could best be established at the outset along the south coast, or, failing that, on the South Downs. The influence of geography on military strategy changes little with time. When British forces occupied the great Iron Age stronghold of Maiden Castle near Dorchester in 1940 as part of the defence against Hitler's Reich the soldiers' curiosity was aroused when they dug out from their weapon pits sling stones, piled up by the Veneti for use against the invading Romans. No doubt they shared the feelings of the Veneti and felt some comradeship with them. Later in the war many Home Guard detachments found themselves in Iron Age or Saxon encampments along the line of hills from Eastbourne to Chichester and on to Golden Cap near Lyme Regis.

The line of the North Downs could be fortified against an invader coming from the south who had successfully broken through the defences of the South Downs. It would be little use however against a force advancing on London the way the Romans had come, along

148

the line of Watling Street. Hence the valley of the Medway must be London's first defence. If that failed the Darent would be the last obstacle before London became exposed to attack. Hence the castle at Rochester and the string of castles along the Darent. But the Mole lies west of London and so no castle was needed there. It is harder to explain why no castle was built to guard the crossing of the Mole itself. Possibly it was more open and thus less vulnerable to ambush or surprise than the crossing places of the other rivers which cut through the North Downs. It does seem however, as if the simple facts of geographical position have conferred upon Box Hill and its surroundings a peacefulness and freedom from violence which have successfully kept it out of the pages of history.

With the coming of the stage coach, followed by the steam engine and later the motor car, the north-south route below Box Hill again became the dominant one. The short time between the popularisation of Brighton as a resort by the Prince Regent and the appearance of the first railways was the golden age of the stage coach. In the Box Hill area there were coaching inns of renown at Burford Bridge and Dorking, with a turnpike gate near the former. The road on which it stood, running through Mickleham and under Box Hill, was not the most important of those which connected London with the south coast. These were the coach road to Portsmouth, which missed Box Hill by going through Guildford, and the main Brighton road which ran a few miles to the east, through Reigate. Nevertheless there were enough travellers going to such places as Dorking and Horsham and on to Chichester to make it worthwhile for the coach proprietors to run several coaches a day by the route below Box Hill. There were also the private carriages of people such as Fanny Burney and Jane Austen and indeed of Horatio Nelson on his detour from the Portsmouth road to say farewell to Lady Hamilton at the old Fox and Hounds Inn, now the Burford Bridge Hotel, before Trafalgar.

There is a note in the "Gentleman's Magazine" of 1787 which provides an interesting instance of the difficulties travellers had to contend with in the pre-railway age. In this note 'An Anonymous Visitor' writes: "Before the turnpike road was made through Epsom, the winter road from the other side of Dorking to London was up the very steep part of Box Hill, the foot of which is near Betchworth Park Gate, and from thence to Sutton." In the largely undrained countryside of the eighteenth century flooding of the river valleys in winter often made the roads through them impassable and alternative routes had to be provided. This winter road over Box Hill avoided the low-lying ground by Burford Bridge. It continued up Juniper Hill, along the line of Stane Street, past Cherkley Court and Tyrrell's Wood. The part of the road which lay up the scarp face of Box Hill can still be made out. It must have been a tremendous pull for the horses. One can readily envisage the scene, with the coachman cracking his whip at the straining team and the more mobile of the passengers skipping alongside, or possibly even being called upon to shove on the worst stretches.

It was the opening of the railways, commencing in the 1840s that put the coachmen out of business. Yet even as late as 1879 fourteen coaches a day were leaving London for destinations as various as Virginia Water, Sevenoaks, Box Hill, Dorking, Guildford and even Brighton. A few brief figures serve to show why the railways so quickly usurped the function of the coaches, bringing about as they did so great social changes. In 1821 the London coach took 5¼ hours to reach Brighton. The fare was £2. In 1851 the same journey by rail took 70 minutes at a fare of 14/6 or 6/-.

The first railway to arrive within sight of Box Hill, in 1849, was the South-eastern and Chatham Company's line from London Bridge via Redhill and Dorking to Reading. The local station, now known as Deepdene, was then actually called Box Hill. The London, Brighton and South Coast line through the Mole gap did not arrive at Box Hill until 1867. The present Box Hill station was built at the same time but was then called West Humble. The construction of this railway completed the domination of the north-south route below Box Hill, for with the coming of the railway came the modern suburb. In the days of horse-drawn transport people could live no further from London than a horse and carriage could comfortably manage to deliver their owner at his London office in time to open the mail and get him home in time for tea. Hence the well-to-do lived at such places as Sydenham, Dulwich, Lewisham and Islington, no more than five miles or so from the City. The railways pushed the suburbs much further out of London. The journey from home to office and back again in the evening could now be comfortably made by the line through the Mole gap, not only from West Humble or Dorking but from places as far away as Bognor and Chichester.

The building of the railways had another important result, that of making the countryside easily and cheaply accessible for men and women in all walks of life. This is well illustrated by a passage from a charming little guide by Walter Miles, "Footpath Rambles Round Dorking", dated 1903. It shows too that the earlier horror of land-lords and nature lovers for the age of steam had changed into some-thing like the affection which now leads to the enthusiastic preserva-tion of country railways such as the Bluebell Line and the Festiniog Railway. Miles writes:

"In West Humble village is the Box Hill Station of the L.B. and S.C. Railway Company. Burford Bridge, by which name the station is also known, will be observed amongst the trees mid-way between the village and the foot of the hill; whilst to the right of the bridge lies the well-known hotel. This is a charming resort, beloved alike by the modest pedestrian and cyclist, as well as those who come down from London in style in a four-in-hand. Men of art and learning found this a peaceful retreat generations back; and it is said that Keats here wrote part of his 'Endymion' . . .

As the sounds of rustic life are borne upon the breeze, the sense of hearing is ever refreshed and gratified. The railway too, which was to spoil our English scenery, but has instead succeeded in adding a romantic charm to its varied attractions, forms a pleasing detail in the scene."

Electrification and nationalisation have done remarkably little to change this assessment since Miles wrote his guide over seventy years ago. Indeed the line by the Mole, with the Southern Electric's green suburban trains rattling along it, is an integral part of a familiar scene, which one would not wish to see disappear. In some ways the railway is a positive advantage where wild life is con-cerned. Effective fencing has made the cuttings and embankments into havens for wild flowers and one or two animals, such as foxes and rabbits. We have seen fascinating glimpses of this wild life by the railway line ourselves on our journeys to and from Box Hill, a fox chased across a field by carrion crows for instance and on one unforgettable occasion, a Hobby, flashing along above the trees by the Mole. The two rail routes, the old South-eastern, following in the vale the line of the Pilgrims' Way above it, and the London, Brighton and South Coast, following that of Stane Street, have done little harm to the sanctuary of Box Hill while making more accessible the play-ground.

Can the same be said of the new motor roads? In so far as they are difficult to leave they do sweep some of the crowds away, down to the coast. The lesser roads, especially the delightful Zig-Zag and the road along the crest of Box Hill, have made the enjoyment of the superb views they command a possibility for the less mobile and the aged. Many a coach-load of senior citizens can renew their youth over a cup of tea at one of the cafés on the summit and a glimpse through the telescope by the Salomon Memorial across the Weald to Chanctonbury. On the other hand there is the menace of the motor-cyclist in his black jacket, interested only in noise and speed, and the frustration of the wanderer by the wayside, compelled to continual scrambling up the banks to avoid the procession of cars which fine evenings and weekends bring forth. It would be churlish, perhaps, to regret this recent development where access to Box Hill is concerned, but it needs careful control. Box Hill now has enough roads.

Amongst the tracks, rather than the roads, on Box Hill, there is one which, though of no great length, is of particular interest. This is the sunken lane which leads uphill to the Fort Café from a point opposite Meredith's house at the foot of the Zig-Zag. It keeps just below the skyline on the north side of the grass slope which is the delight of skiers in those rare winters like that of 1962-63 when Burford Bridge becomes a winter sports centre. This green road, with the immediate release it affords from the importunate motor cars on the Zig-Zag, was a great delight to us. We followed it many times, to admire flocks of greenfinches twittering in the thorn trees, or redwings and fieldfares amongst the yews of the far slope in winter, or the glistening whitebeams in spring, orchids and low-flying swifts in summer. At all times of the year there is something interesting to see there. It was not until we read Geoffrey Hutchings' "Book of Box Hill" however that we discovered that this peaceful haunt of rock-rose and clustered bellflower, blue butterflies and chiffchaffs, was known as the Military Road. We had always thought that it was quite old, perhaps a spur of the Pilgrims' Way. In this we were wrong, as we also were about the age of the old fort to which it leads. This we had always thought to be a relic of the Napoleonic wars, situated there for the same reason as the Martello towers are situated on the south coast, to repel a possible French invasion. However, both lane and fort were constructed no longer ago than the 1880s, when Parliament, shocked out of its complacency by the easy victory of Prussia in the Franco-Prussian War, set about considering how Volunteer Defence along the line of the North Downs might serve as long-stop to the Fleet and the first defence line of the South

152

Downs should the inconceivable happen and the Fleet suffer defeat at the hands of French or German or Russian naval power. General Sir E. Hamley first raised the matter and when Lord Salisbury replaced Gladstone as Prime Minister in 1880 the new Conservative Government authorised the purchase of sites for twelve of these forts on the North Downs between Knockholt and Guildford. They were constructed for heavy guns but no guns were ever mounted in them though a field of fire was cleared through the trees on the top of Box Hill. In 1905 the change to a Liberal Government and the launching of the first Dreadnought combined to restore belief in the efficiency of the Navy. In consequence the provision of land fortresses was seen as an unnecessary extravagance and the policy which had led to the construction of the forts and of our Military Road, was discontinued. The Box Hill site was sold back to the original owner, complete with fort and the Military Road left to the flowers and the birds.

An important event in bringing about the change of policy in 1880 and so, indirectly, providing the delightful Nature Trail of the Military Road, was the publication in "Blackwood's Magazine" of May 1871, of a remarkable article entitled "The Battle of Dorking — Reminiscences of a Volunteer". It is a vivid account of an imaginary great defeat of British forces in a battle for the Mole gap, following a successful German invasion of the south coast after the Fleet had been destroyed. It is an extremely graphic, almost frightening, description of the impossible, the defeat of Britain on her own soil, coming true. The convincing nature of the story owes much to the accurate knowledge of local topography displayed by the writer. One can easily identify the features in the landscape where various actions take place and follow the imaginary battle, phase by phase, from the moment when the first desultory shots are fired to the bitter climax when the shattered Volunteer Regiment to which the author belongs, vainly attempts to reform on the heights of Ranmore. The writer, Sir George Chesney, plainly knew the lie of the land well. The tactics of the defenders are those which a military expert might have expected would be employed in the years between the Franco-Prussian and Boer Wars. The soldiers still wore full regimentals of scarlet and blue. Bands played them into battle. Yet the story rings true and it jerked many people out of their complacency at the time. It is the most important event which NEVER happened on Box Hill. A battle of any kind there, let alone one of such dimensions, would be a bad dream indeed. Nevertheless, the forts on the top of Box Hill and on Ranmore, where another was sited, along with the pill boxes of the Home Guard, which still stand on the face of the escarpment, are mute witnesses to the fact that the nightmare could have become a reality.

There are other reminders of the Second World War on Box Hill. Below the line of pill boxes along the Pilgrims' Way a strip of earth was clawed clear and steepened to serve as a tank obstacle. This bare strip was clearly visible as late as the 1950s, being marked by a change of vegetation half-way up the slope where the chalk had been exposed, to nettles, thistles, wild mignonette and other quick-growing plants, contrasting sharply with the established matted chalk flora of the rest of the slope. It took the orchids twenty years to re-colonise the area from which they had been bull-dozed in 1940. There is the rifle range above Wotton where, for some unexplained reason, the chalkland flowers grow to great size, guarded by the bullets and red flags of the Territorial Army. More comical is the bomb crater on the scarp above Brockham in which some botanist with a taste for practical joking sowed seeds of foreign plants. When these germinated there was quite a lengthy correspondence in the press about the chances of the seeds having arrived in the bomb which made the crater.

Perhaps the most interesting of the memorials of the last war are the least well-known. These lie, hidden from view, in the enormous chalk quarry above Betchworth. To this quarry, early in 1944, shortly before the invasion of Normandy, one* of us who was personally involved recounts, we brought over fifty Churchill tanks. They were brand-new and all ready for water-proofing for the beaches but we had never been able to find out if the 75mm guns actually recoiled and ran out properly when fired. Since an armour-piercing shell, with a muzzle-velocity approaching 3000 feet per second, bounces up to ten miles, there were precious few places in England where the guns could be fired without damage to the population and these were hundreds of track-miles away. We could not afford the wear and tear on the tracks, engines and gear boxes of the journey to one of these far-away ranges if the tanks were to last through the Normandy campaign. Some genius thought of the Betchworth quarries and we solemnly trundled our fifty-odd tanks from beyond Haslemere and through Dorking to fire off each gun at

* Bob Young.

154

point-blank range into the soft Lower Chalk at Betchworth. Here there could be no ricochet as there would have been at the tank range at Warcop in Westmorland. No blocks of steel would bounce onto the Crystal Palace or Epsom ridges. They were all safely embedded in the chalk and we went back to Haslemere assured that the guns would work. Apart from occasional pilots bailing out and odd "doodle bugs" gone astray, this was probably as close as Box Hill got to World War Two.

So the history of Box Hill ends as it began with nothing of great consequence to record but rather a message of peace. Its history is the history of the lives of simple men, men like Pepys' old shepherd and his little son. Neolithic hunters and herdsmen, petty Roman officials and Romano-British middlemen, prowling Saxons looking for land of good quality on which to establish their farms, shepherds and woodmen, the gallants who incurred Defoe's displeasure, coachmen and turnpike keepers, such were the people whose lives compose the history of Box Hill. They were men like ourselves who felt the clean winds of the scarp face, smelt the sharp tang of the chalk sward, listened to the song of the lark ascending, men who rarely saw life in terms of their own death. Yet they did die and their names are forgotten. They were the "humble men" of whom Ecclesiasticus wrote, "which have no memorial". Yet one is conscious of their having lived what were, in the main, valuable and useful lives here. One sees the results of their work all around one on Box Hill; feels that something of them survives in it. Because of them it remains "a goodly inheritance". It is this which is their memorial and, in the triumphant words with which Ecclesiasticus dismisses his earlier fatalistic view of man's insignificance, "their glory shall not be blotted out."

CHAPTER TWELVE
TREES, WOODLAND AND FORESTRY ON BOX HILL

Beech

From whatever direction one approaches Box Hill, or wherever one walks on it, one cannot fail to be delighted by the number and variety of the trees. There are the scattered yews, dark and compact of form, on the escarpment; the thickets of the aromatic box, which gives the hill its name, on the steep slopes of the Whites; the little platoons of birch trees deployed on the ascent to Juniper Top; the whitebeams which mark the curving track of the Military Road up the western side of the Zig-Zag, opposite Meredith's house; the steep-pitching beech hanger which drops to the Headley Lane near Warren Farm; the single file of alders, limes, poplars, sycamores, horse chestnuts and willows along the banks of the Mole between Burford Bridge and the Weypole; above all there are the soaring grey trunks and spreading fans of leaves of the beeches which are found in stately groves in many places on Box Hill. These beautiful trees induce in one's mind a contentment which is increased by the manner in which they emphasise the satisfying contours of the landscape and by the contrast they provide with the jumbled mass of roofs and chimney pots of south London and the neatly ordered ranks of the houses of suburbia, seen from the train on its way to Box Hill.

156

The trees of Box Hill do more than contribute greatly to the beauty of the landscape. They play an important part in the creation of the indefinable, almost magical, atmosphere of the place. For example, following the path along the crest of White Hill one comes to a point near Cherkley Wood where the ground drops steeply into a narrow combe. The combe is bordered by tall trees of peculiarly arresting shape. They seem to be leaning forward, as if listening or watching. Below these trees the eye is led across the Headley Valley into another combe. This trends up the slope, past Wentworth Hall, to the fringe of trees which marks the eastern edge of Ashurst Rough. It resembles the backdrop for some pastoral play, idealised and larger than life. Oberon and Titania, Bottom the Weaver and Flute the Bellows-mender, would feel at home here. It would come as no surprise if Herne the Hunter, in his coat of green, were to emerge quietly upon the scene. Without the trees however it is doubtful if this beautiful piece of the landscape would have the power to grip the imagination in this way.

The tree landscape of Box Hill is almost entirely the result of man's handiwork. Much of it is the product of careful planning. It is an example of the way in which man can embellish nature, for nearly all of it is the outcome of either his clearing and felling or of his planting. Elsewhere one comes upon places where the former activities might be more accurately described as axing and smashing, with disastrous results for the landscape. Fortunately, on Box Hill there is no sign of this sort of thing. The planting and the careful forestry practised there have had almost uniformly happy results from the time when the box was managed as a crop for the production of box-wood and men made their furniture from beech and oak rather than plastics. One sees all around the results of those periods in the past when it was fashionable to plant trees. These were mainly in the latter half of the seventeenth century and the first half of the eighteenth. This was the Romantic Age, in which men sought to create picturesque landscapes by careful siting of trees, either individually or in groups. It was during these years that Sir Cecil Bishopp and Joseph Bonsor were planting their trees on the Juniper Hall and Polesden Lacy estates. The latter is said to have planted the astonishing total of 20,000 trees in the years 1824 and 1825 alone. John Evelyn, the diarist, whose famous work "Sylva, or a Discourse of Forest Trees", published in 1664, was the first book written in English to encourage land-owners to plant trees, was born at Wotton, not far from Dorking and went back to live there in his old age. He would have been pleased to see the wealth of trees on and around Box Hill today.

The agricultural practices of the farmers in past years had also an important influence on the tree landscape of Box Hill. They cleared and cultivated the good soil of the bottoms and lower sides of the valleys. The thin soils of the upper slopes and the escarpment they maintained as sheep pastures. The sheep and their allies the rabbits kept the scrub and its natural successor, the woodland, at bay, so here the traditional downland landscape of short-cropped sward prevailed. The stiff, intractable Clay-with-Flints which overlies the plateau-like tops of the North Downs was however, usually left to grow the trees and shrubs which are natural to it. The practice formed a necessary part of the rural economy of former times. It resulted in a semi-managed type of woodland known as coppice-with-standards, consisting of a number of large trees, chiefly oaks, and a considerable quantity of undergrowth in which hazel predominated. The oaks provided timber for constructional purposes, chiefly the building of houses, farmsteads and out-houses while the hazel was regularly cropped to supply such things as hop and bean poles, hurdles and the like. Today, when timber for buildings comes largely from overseas and wire netting has replaced wattle hurdles, these woodlands often stand neglected and many of them are falling into slow decay. Another reason for this is that nowadays few landowners are able to afford the expense of keeping their woodlands in good order. However where woodlands are the property of the National Trust, as they are on Box Hill, they are properly cared for and the replanting which is necessary for their continued existence, expertly carried out.

The woodlands of Box Hill are therefore largely the outcome of man's utilisation of the possibilities the locality offers for profit and pleasure by the growing of trees. The character of the soil of course has an important influence on the type of tree which grows on it. Chalk favours beech, yew and whitebeam, Clay-with-Flints oak, holly and birch, though both beech and ash grow well on it. Of natural woodland in the strict sense of the word no vestige remains except possibly in one small area. This is the woodland on the Whites, above the Mole between Burford Bridge and the Weypole. Here, on slopes too steep for even sheep to graze, there grows a mixture of trees, principally beech, yew and box, with underlying shrubs and plants such as elder, honeysuckle and wild clematis. This association of species appears able to re-seed itself successfully over the years so that its character never varies. The tangled woodland of the Whites may look much the same today as it did when Stone Age hunters roamed the banks of the Mole.

Certain species of trees, chiefly beech, box, yew and whitebeam, are dominant on Box Hill because they are tolerant of a limey soil. Another lime-loving tree, the ash, is less common there. This is perhaps surprising, especially to those who know the limestone country of the Pennines where the ash is the commonest tree. There however, the ash has a running start over the beech. It has lighter seeds than the beech, an initial advantage on those windswept hills. Its seedlings grow faster than those of the beech but its leaves open later, avoiding damage from late spring frosts. An example of the vigour with which the ash can speedily dominate its environment may be seen in Dovedale, on the borders of Derbyshire and Staffordshire. Here, since the drastic diminution of the rabbit population following the myxomatosis outbreak removed the chief enemy of the ash seedlings, the tree has spread with great speed. In the North Downs however, the beech, once established, seems to have the power to suppress the ash, as it does most other forms of vegetation, large and small, with the exception of box and yew and plants such as dog's mercury and violet, which flower and seed early in the spring before the beech leaves have opened and shut out the light. After this has happened very little will be found growing beneath the beeches save certain species of orchids, such as the white helleborine and even these are poor and stunted, especially where the shade is deepest. Where both the creation and the tolerance of shade are concerned the beech is manifestly more powerful than the ash. As G.E. Hutchings has pointed out in "The Book of Box Hill", beech seedlings can grow steadily, regardless of shade cast by their neighbours while the ash tolerates shade much less readily. Ash seedlings cannot survive in the low-light intensity of beech woods with the result that, even if present originally, the ash fails to reproduce itself. A struggle between beech and ash may be observed to be in progress at the present time around the old fort at the top of Box Hill, though here the ash has received some assistance from the woodman's axe in the past. Single ash trees may be found in the woodlands on the Clay-with-Flints where the tree was often grown as a standard along with the oak. Here it was not in competition with

159

the beech. In the one place on Box Hill where ash trees grow in any number, at the head of the perhaps significantly named Ashurst Valley, there are few beech trees and the ash is able to flourish.

After the beech the yew is the most characteristic tree of the Box Hill woodlands. Like the box it can tolerate the shade of the beeches and most beech woods contain a few yew trees. They grow slowly but to a great age. One does not have to walk far on Box Hill to find large yews which are obviously very old. There are others in the woods on the Norbury side of the Mole valley, particularly in the area known as the Druids' Grove. In many parts of Box Hill the yew trees grow alone. In others they form small but dense thickets. One such thicket, on the western side of Juniper Top, is so extensive as to be more deserving of the description of forest. Here the yews have virtually suppressed all other forms of vegetation and the ground beneath them is bare. On those occasions when we found ourselves abroad on the hill in a gale of wind or drenching rain, the yew forest provided both safety from crashing branches and shelter from the rain. In the latter case it was advisable not to sit with one's back against the trunk of one of the yews because eventually rainwater would come trickling down it from the top of the tree. It was quite good fun, provided one had time to wait for the storm to pass, to sit snugly on the dry ground beneath the natural umbrella of the yews, watching the grey curtains of rain drifting across the distant prospect and listening to the roar of the wind in the tall trees at the top of the hill. Yew trees seldom break under the most testing conditions imposed by rough weather though they may be scorched by severe frost. For years after the fierce winter of 1962-63 the yew trees in Juniper Bottom were brown and withered on the side from which the killing arctic winds had come.

Oaks grow well on clays and loams but not on chalk or limestone. Thus one does not find oaks growing on the pure chalk areas of Box Hill. They are to be found however where the Clay with Flints overlies the chalk, as in Ashurst Rough. Oaks grow slowly. Nor do they cast the heavy shade which beech and yew both do. This permits a vigorous undergrowth to flourish beneath them. Such low-growing shrubs as hazel, holly, elderberry, bramble and honeysuckle, are all to be found growing beneath the oaks of Ashurst Rough. Of the many plants which constitute the ground layer here, the most beautiful is the bluebell. In May there is an azure carpet beneath the grey stems of the hazels and the gnarled bark of the trunks of the oaks while the delicate fragrance of the bluebells fills the air. Amongst them one sees at times less beauteous sights, the broad rumps, like enormous toadstools, of the bluebell pickers. It may seem unkind to deny to people the traditional pleasure of taking home a bunch of bluebells from a Sunday outing but there is no doubt that the heavy picking to which the bluebells are subjected in woods which are popular resorts will mean eventually no bluebells for anyone.

Birch, beech, holly and yew all grow with oaks. In some parts of Ashurst Rough the beech has become dominant and has crowded out other trees, if any grew there originally. Some of the finest groves of beeches on Box Hill are to be found here, places of supreme beauty, where the silvery-grey trunks rise upwards, straight and true, for thirty feet or more before the first long branches with their delicate green leaves fan out from the main trunk. On hot summer evenings it is cool in these groves. The sunlight slants down in long golden shafts through gaps in the leaf canopy overhead, illuminating the floor of brown dead leaves or mossy grass with patches of flickering light. They are the most beautiful places in the Box Hill woods.

In other parts of Ashurst Rough, for example near the caravan park, the oak is dominant. Even where it has no competitors however, the oak does not grow to any size on Box Hill. There are no great oaks such as those of Sherwood or Woodstock. When the trees are from eighty to one hundred years old, a comparatively short time in the life of an oak, their roots penetrate the layer of Clay-with-Flints and reach the underlying chalk. When this happens the trees lose their vigour and begin to deteriorate. The beeches, in contrast, continue to grow with uninterrupted strength when their roots reach the chalk. The danger point in the life of a beech is in the early stages of its growth, when it is particularly vulnerable to attack from that chief of woodland pests the grey squirrel. The damage done by these animals is not always apparent to the casual observer but to the forester it is only too obvious. The bark is gnawed from the trunk of the growing tree after which nothing can save it. Young beeches on Box Hill and other parts of the North Downs have suffered badly in recent years from damage of this kind. Trees are vulnerable to the age of at least forty years. While it is possible to protect a sapling with a guard there is no way of protecting the bigger tree except by removing the squirrels. This is a problem which has not yet been solved though the animals' numbers can be kept down by shooting and trapping them.

Man-made conifer plantations have not invaded Box Hill in the same way that they have Leith Hill and some of its neighbours. The chalk is, perhaps fortunately, not a rock on which many of the conifers thrive whereas the acidic greensand of the Leith Hill range is. Nevertheless some experiments in growing conifers on Box Hill have been tried. In 1875 larches and Scots pines were introduced on the flat top of Lodge Hill, in parts of Ashurst Rough and on the western side of Juniper Bottom. These areas are capped with Clay-with-Flints and the trees grew well. Many of them were felled during the two world wars and only a few now remain. There is, for instance, an isolated group of Scots pines on Lodge Hill, near the northern end of the ride which leads from the top of Box Hill, near to the old fort. One comes upon them with mild surprise after walking through what is otherwise entirely deciduous woodland. A little further along is the largest group of conifers of mature size in this part of Box Hill, the shelter belt of pines above Pinehurst, looking down on Meredith's house.

Between the wars the National Trust, in association with the Forestry Commission, planted more conifers on Lodge Hill. In 1928 they experimented with larch and Scots pine in Juniper Bottom. There is a small group of larches, now grown fairly tall, halfway up this valley. They make a pleasing addition to the scene and are an attraction to coal tits and goldcrests. One would not, however, wish to see more than a small number of these trees. They are alien to the chalk and, in the mass, would look out of place. At present the planting of conifers on Box Hill is confined to a small number of rectangular blocks of larch and pine which are safely tucked away out of sight in the depths of Ashurst Rough or concealed by broad belts of tall deciduous trees on Lodge Hill. The few little groups of conifers which do stand out in the open, such as the Scots pines on Lodge Hill and the larches in Juniper Bottom are quite an acceptable addition to the tree landscape of Box Hill. Like the birch trees which grow beside the track leading to Juniper Top, they bring a whiff of the wildness of the Highlands of Scotland to these soft south country hills.

The woodlands on and near Box Hill, though they may appear natural and indeed wild and lonely in places, are in fact good examples of managed woodlands. The greater part of them are in the care of the National Trust whose declared policy is, in the Trust's own words, to ensure that "there will always be beautiful trees for future generations to enjoy.'' The efficient management of woodland involves the cutting down of trees as well as the planting of new ones. The trees which were planted by men like Sir Cecil Bishopp and Joseph Bonsor two centuries ago are now old. Many are past their prime, some even dead or dying. They must be felled and replaced if the tree landscape of Box Hill is to remain as beautiful in the future as it is today.

Nevertheless it is always with a sense of shock, possibly even with outrage, that one comes across some corner of the woodland which one has known, perhaps for many years, to find that the trees there have been felled. The bringing to earth of tall trees is always a drastic business, however carefully and efficiently done. Undergrowth is broken and flattened, sawdust litters the ground, neatly stacked piles of logs stand at the edges of the new clearing, the ashes of fires show where the useless trash has been burned. The trunks of the trees which have been felled have disappeared. Deep ruts in the soft forest earth mark where they have been hauled away. All this one regards with dismay. Perhaps it was a grove where the Wood Warbler sometimes sang in May or one came across flocks of bramblings in winter. Perhaps it was a place where one had found particular joy in solitude or just a favourite spot where one had liked to lie and see the summer sky through the leaves. Good forestry however necessitates such measure from time to time. Trees, like men, have their allotted span. Though it is a good idea to leave a few dead trees for the woodpeckers to enjoy and the titmice and nuthatches to find nest holes, future generations would hold us responsible if we handed on to them a collection of aged and rotting forest veterans with storm-shattered limbs and fungus-covered trunks. In properly managed woodlands there is always a continuous programme of felling and re-planting. Visit the part of the wood where trees have been felled in a year or two and the chances are that one will find small trees, each one enclosed in its deer and squirrel-proof cage, growing sturdily amongst the stumps of their predecessors. As a bonus one has the excitement of finding a variety of wild flowers, whose seeds had lain dormant in the earth beneath the trees which have been felled, growing where one had never expected them to be.

We shall not live to see these infant trees grow to maturity. But future generations will and maybe think with gratitude of those who planted them. The planting of a tree, other than one of the few fast-growing species which approach maturity in less than half a century, is one of the most selfless acts which anyone can perform for in doing it he affirms his own mortality. The deciduous forest trees of Britain, oak, beech, lime, elm and ash, take more than a century to grow to their full size and greatest beauty. To plant one of them is to share in the pleasure of generations yet unborn. Just as we, contemplating with delight, the magnificent trees of the Mole valley and Box Hill, Polesden Lacy and Denbies, think gratefully of the men who planted them, so will others in years to come, be grateful for the work of the National Trust and other land owners in the woodlands on and around Box Hill.

There are few rare or unusual trees on Box Hill. Where any do occur they are the result, as a rule, of experiments carried out by private land-owners in the past. Hutchings mentions several scarlet oaks growing at the south end of Lodge Hill. There are specimens of the western hemlock and fastigiate beech in the same area. Some sweet gums (luquidambar) and Cappadocian maples were planted on the western side of Juniper Bottom and in Ashurst Rough in 1929. There are a number of exotic trees in the Weypole and beside the Mole in the near-by meadows. This is not surprising when it is remembered that Burford Lodge was the home, some seventy years ago, of Sir Trevor Lawrence, Baronet, a noted horticulturalist and one-time President of the Royal Horticultural Society. Sir Trevor delighted in experimenting with the introduction of foreign trees and plants to England. As the grounds of the Lodge stretched to the Mole in his day it is possible that some of these trees were put there by him.

The Weypole seems to have been at some time a garden or orchard for some old apple and cherry trees grow there. So also did a fine walnut until it fell down a few years ago, to the great regret of the nuthatches which used to run up and down its gnarled limbs and quite possibly nested in them as we often saw parties of young ones about them in the summer. A few hornbeams also grow in the Weypole. The nuts of this tree are a favourite food of the Hawfinch which may account for the occasional appearance here of this most furtive of the finches. Copper beech, weeping willow and sycamore, growing by the Mole or in the meadows between the river and Burford Lodge, are other trees which may have been introduced to this locality.

Box Hill is therefore no arboretum, though the fact that it possesses one of the only three natural box woods in England gives it considerable distinction in the eyes of the botanist. Its trees and woods are, for the most part, those which are characteristic of the North Downs as a whole. They constitute an indispensable component of the Box Hill landscape and are, in great measure, responsible for its supreme beauty. It is a reassuring thought for those who love the Hill, that under the wise management of the National Trust, this situation is most unlikely to be changed.

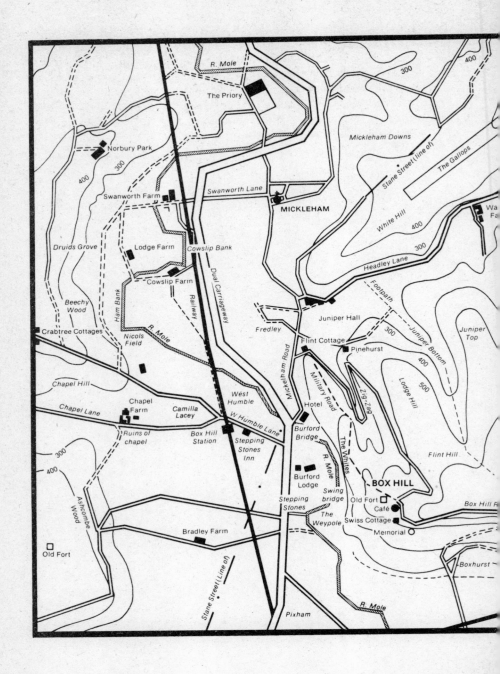

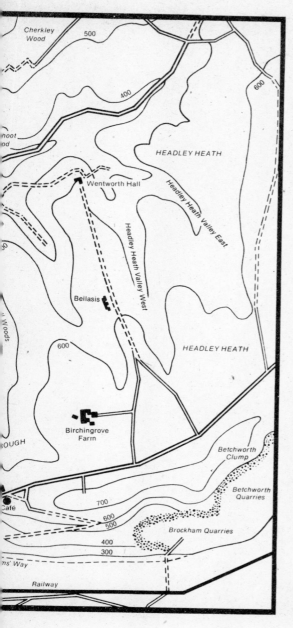

Cherkley Wood

500

400

600

noot
od

HEADLEY HEATH

Wentworth Hall

Headley Heath Valley East

Headley Heath Valley West

Bellasis

600

HEADLEY HEATH

Woods

Birchingrove Farm

Betchworth Clump

OUGH

Betchworth Quarries

Café

700

600
500

Brockham Quarries

400
300

ns' Way

Railway

"Generalised sketch map of the Box Hill area to show places mentioned in the text.

Based on the 1:25,000 Ordnance Survey map but not to scale.

A minimum number of contour lines is shown, sufficient to indicate main areas of high and low ground and to show the lie of the land.

Only a small number of the numerous tracks and foot-paths in the area is shown. To show more would be confusing on such a small map. The reader is recommended to refer to the Ordnance Survey maps of the area which show them all, though it should be noted that they are not all necessarily rights of way."

NOTES